ANDY MCILREE

Seeing the Best in Scripture's Women of Worth

HAYES
PRESS Christian Publisher

First edition

This book was professionally typeset on Reedsy.
Find out more at reedsy.com

Contents

Chapter 1: Introduction   1

Chapter 2: Sarah   5

Chapter 2 Questions   16

Chapter 3: Overlooked Women – Part 1   17

Chapter 3 Questions   27

Chapter 4: Overlooked Women – Part 2   28

Chapter 4 Questions   39

Chapter 5: Deborah   40

Chapter 5 Questions   51

Chapter 6: Abigail   52

Chapter 6 Questions   65

Chapter 7: A Certain Woman   68

Chapter 7 Questions   78

Chapter 8: A Notable Woman   79

Chapter 8 Questions   90

Chapter 9: Choice Women   91

Chapter 9 Questions   105

Chapter 10: Building Women   106

Chapter 10 Questions   117

Chapter 11: The Woman at the Well   118

Chapter 11 Questions   128

Chapter 12: An Infirm Woman   129

Chapter 12 Questions   139

Chapter 13: Phoebe   140

Chapter 13 Questions   152

Chapter 14: Women in Church   153

Chapter 14 Questions   165

Chapter 15: Mary – the Lord's Mother   166

Chapter 16: Conclusion   177

Appendix   184

REFERENCES   189

ABOUT THE AUTHOR   193

MORE BOOKS FROM THE AUTHOR   194

ABOUT THE PUBLISHER   199

Chapter 1: Introduction

One thing is clear in our Bibles: God calls women. They take their place – often standing beside His men, sometimes even prepared to stand without them. Irrespective of their circumstances, they all knew something about the heart of their God: He never patronises them. Because of that, they fitted in where He set them and, even in the most difficult situations, they undoubtedly felt comfortable in their role.

Do you? Can you honestly say that you are spiritually comfortable, that you feel at home, truly at ease in your particular sphere? God's women are called to feel right with Him, right with themselves, and right with others. That's what He wanted all along. It's what He still wants, and He wants the same for you. Is this how you feel with God, with yourself and with your church? How is it possible?

First of all, He is interested in the character of His women. Look at how He describes them in the New Testament:

- Mark 15:41 – Ministering women
- Luke 8:2 – Certain women
- Luke 23:49 – Following women
- Acts 16:13 – Praying women

1

- 1 Timothy 2:10 - Godly women
- Titus 2:3-5 - Teaching women
- 1 Peter 3:5 - Holy women

These are His words that show the perfect appreciation the Perfect One had of them. They are His inspired words, each of them intended to sanctify and satisfy His inspired women. Did you notice the order? Sanctified, then satisfied. Whatever your aim is, whatever service you feel is cut out for you, you will never have satisfaction without sanctification. Long before God brought His people into the land of Canaan, well ahead of going through the Jordan into the place of victories by faith, He spoke to them in Numbers 6:2 about this matter of being wholly dedicated to Him: *"When either a man or woman consecrates an offering to take the vow of a Nazirite, to separate himself to the LORD."*

Man or woman! She was side-by-side in her femininity, side-by-side in her spirituality, and side-by-side in opportunity. That's the lesson. And, throughout the New Testament, these seven descriptions – ministering, certain, following, praying, Godly, teaching, holy – all emphasise that God is still the God of consecrated women.

Is this what you would like to be? Would you like to be sure about your spiritual direction? In response to what He would like you to be, will you consider making a vow? It's a pledge that affects your devotion, your dedication and the duration of your life. Whenever you take care of these three, He will take care of the direction. You look after your character and He will look after your contribution! That's His part. He is the God of the open door and He's the One who holds the door open for His women. Not men! They are meant to go together, of course. Just as it was in Nehemiah's day (see chapter 3:12), men and women are expected to work together as mutual encouragers of God-given opportunity and Spirit-led maturity. Psalm 144:12 describes this rather aptly. *"That our sons may be as plants grown up in their youth; that our daughters may be as pillars, sculptured in palace style."*

Much is said about women's subjection, but part of a man's subjection is to acknowledge and assist a woman's role, thus honouring her subjection. His role is what could be called 'assisted consecration' and part of this will be to ensure that she is helped to recognise God's opened doors. So let's look at some of the doors He may open for you:

- Deborah: Leading (Judg.4:8,9; 5:15)
- Ruth: Subjecting (Ruth 3:1-7)
- Abigail: Advising (1 Sam.25:23-31)
- Shallum's daughters: Building (Neh.3:12)
- Phoebe: Protecting (Rom.16:1,2)
- Tryphena & Tryphosa: Labouring (Rom.16:12)
- Euodia & Syntyche: Witnessing (Phil.4:2,3)

Once again, seven examples combine to show what God thinks of His women. They are:

- Women of His worth,
- Women of His Word, and
- Women of His Work.

Consecrated women are all three! Along with these, by His help, they learn to appreciate and appropriate their femininity, their womanhood, and, as Psalm 128:3 so beautifully points out, their motherhood too. *"Your wife shall be like a fruitful vine in the very heart of your house, your children like olive plants all around your table."* But questions automatically arise:

- How does a woman currently fulfil a leadership role?
- How applicable is Ruth's subjection to 21st century women?
- Does such an external witness as long hair still count?
- How do present-day Abigails fulfil an advisory role and live up to her name as 'sources of joy'?
- How can women be effective and successful builders?
- How was Phoebe enabled to be such a protector and so valued a servant? (Gr. *prostatis*: protectress. "Prostatēs was the title of a citizen of Athens who had the responsibility of seeing to the welfare of resident aliens who were without civil rights." W. E. Vine)
- How did Tryphena and Tryphosa get so worn out? They were 'Dainty' and 'Delicate' yet toiling to the point of exhaustion.
- How did Euodia and Syntyche wrestle in the gospel with Paul, as if they were sharing his struggle and contest?

Each of these questions deserves our thoughtful attention, so that godly sisters can more fully serve their God in the company of godly brethren – 'Men God Moved' in fellowship with 'Women God Moved'!

Chapter 2: Sarah

"Sarah lived one hundred and twenty-seven years; these were the years of the life of Sarah. So Sarah died in Kirjath Arba (that is, Hebron) in the land of Canaan, and Abraham came to mourn for Sarah and to weep for her. Then Abraham stood up from before his dead, and spoke to the sons of Heth, saying, 'I am a foreigner and a visitor among you. Give me property for a burial place among you, that I may bury my dead out of my sight.' And the sons of Heth answered Abraham, saying to him, "Hear us, my lord: You are a mighty prince among us; bury your dead in the choicest of our burial places. None of us will withhold from you his burial place, that you may bury your dead"' (Gen.23:1-6).

"Do not let your adornment be merely outward—arranging the hair, wearing gold, or putting on fine apparel— rather let it be the hidden person of the heart, with the incorruptible beauty of a gentle and quiet spirit, which is very precious in the sight of God. For in this manner, in former times, the holy women who trusted in God also adorned themselves, being submissive to their own husbands, as Sarah obeyed Abraham, calling him lord, whose daughters you are if you do good and are not afraid with any terror" (1 Pet.3:3-6).

T wo great biblical precepts lie behind the lives of Abraham and Sarah: in his willingness to offer up Isaac, he gave a poignant foreshadowing of Christ, while Sarah became a vivid foreshadowing of Christlikeness. Because of this, their marriage and lifetime together marked them out as compatible people, but, more than that, they were a marriage of complementary principles. The New Testament testifies to both: firstly, in Romans 4:11 which refers to him as being *"the father of all those who believe,"* and in verse 16 as *"the father of us all."*

Although this points to Abraham's place in the purpose of God, God would achieve it through the sacrifice of His Son who would come to fulfil God's promise to Abraham, *"In Isaac your seed shall be called."* In the cross of Christ, God has shown that He was the one He had in mind as the Seed while, at the same time, fulfilling two other vital aspects. As the sacrifice for sin, He is the Seed of the woman;[1] as the substitute on the cross, He is the Seed of Abraham;[2] and as Sovereign on the throne, He is the Seed of David.[3] These, and these alone, allow each genuinely born again believer to say, "He is my Saviour, my Substitute, and my King."

Outside of Genesis, Isaiah is the only other Old Testament book in which God mentions Sarah, and He did it to link Abraham's role as His people's father and hers as their mother.[4] This is rather striking, since Peter had a similar objective as he drew lessons from her for Christian wives, though, as we shall see, much of what he said applies to all godly women, married or single. So much could be said about her by confining ourselves to the book of Genesis to trace the evidence of the hand of God in her life. We might conclude from chapter 12 that she was in the background of God's purpose when Abram was called to leave his homeland, but both had their names changed in chapter

17, which shows that God was as interested in her identity as He was in his. This was further enhanced in the blessing that followed with the promise that a son would be only the beginning of her motherhood of nations and kings.

In chapter 18, Abraham included Sarah in his rush to welcome and refresh three unexpected heavenly visitors, one of whom was the Lord. It is noticeable in verse 9 that together they used her new name and said to him, *"Where is Sarah your wife?"* As soon as Abraham replied, the Lord spoke on his own, and she paid attention to the voice of omniscience as He announced, *"I will certainly return to you according to the time of life, and behold, Sarah your wife shall have a son."* Undoubtedly, she was still listening when He added, *"Is anything too hard for the LORD?"* Now she knew, this was Jehovah at her tent door repeating His promise: *"At the appointed time I will return to you, according to the time of life, and Sarah shall have a son."* Could her faith ever be more tested than this?

There is no mention of her in chapter 22, as father and son left home for their journey to Moriah for the greatest test of all when he *"offered up his only begotten son, of whom it was said, 'In Isaac your seed shall be called,' concluding that God was able to raise him up, even from the dead, from which he also received him in a figurative sense."*[5] We are not told if she knew beforehand or came to know afterward, but tracing her experience with God in Genesis leaves us in no doubt that her life was shaped by faith. With this background at the forefront of our minds, we consider Peter's estimation of her knowing that it rests on the word of the Inspirer whom she heard at her tent door.

The hidden person

Apart from all we are able to read about Sarah, there was part of her that only God could read and only He could make known. Peter calls it *"the hidden person of the heart,"* which is unseen by the human eye yet visible to God. Paul refers to it as *"the inward man"* that delights in the law of God in Romans 7:22 and contrasts its daily renewal with the gradual decay of the body in 2 Corinthians 4:16. It is the inner being, the soul, which, in believers, responds to the communication and prompting of the Holy Spirit and then enables us to glorify God in our bodies.[6] The soul, as the eternal and spiritual part of us, therefore becomes stronger while the body, as the temporal and physical part, becomes weaker. It is this inward and hidden person of the heart that engages with God by faith, which both hears and receives *"with meekness the implanted word"*[7] and allows *"the word of Christ to dwell in* [us] *richly."*[8] The inner working of God's Spirit through the Word makes us spiritually what we are, and then produces evidence in what we do.

Paul beautifully emphasises this progression in the next verse: *"And whatever you do in word or deed, do all in the name of the Lord Jesus, giving thanks to God the Father through Him."* The truth is, of course, that verse 17 is impossible without the inward experience of verse 16. The visible and audible can never testify without an invisible and inaudible work of God. To put it simply, we cannot work outwardly for God unless and until He has worked inwardly for us! Had God not seen this in Sarah, He couldn't have shown it to Peter.

Incorruptible beauty

When Abram took Sarai to Egypt, he was concerned that her beauty would be an unwelcomed distraction and that his only means of survival would be in saying she was his sister. It was partly true for she was his stepsister,[9] but it wasn't as true as saying she was his wife. At that point, prior to her name change, some have suggested that Sarai included the thought of contention or dominion, but there was never any indication that her temperament was tainted in such a negative way. On the contrary, the aptly named Sarah – princess – is regal in her demeanour and deportment with her "heart" and "spirit" at one. Fingers have pointed accusingly at her for laughing "within herself," but who would have known had the omniscient LORD not divulged it?

Abraham also laughed when he thought of the improbability of a couple having a child when their average age was ninety-five, and Sarah laughed openly when Isaac – meaning laughter – was born. This time, *"Sarah said, 'God has made me laugh, and all who hear will laugh with me.' She also said, 'Who would have said to Abraham that Sarah would nurse children? For I have borne him a son in his old age.'"*[10] Is there not a great gulf between laughing at the improbable and mocking the impossible? Human nature made her do the first, but the inward working of the divine nature kept her from the second! She certainly didn't forfeit the inner characteristics of a mild, humble and peaceable spirit that are of great value in the eyes of God.

Holy women who trusted in God

God's commendation of Sarah through Peter allows us to trace her life with Abraham and view her own sensitivity and submission to His will. Unlike Job's wife, she was not the kind of woman who struck out at God when events tested her patience. Scripture speaks about *"the perseverance of Job,"*[11] but the same could not be said of her when, in a hot-headed outburst, she lashed out, *"Curse God and die!"*[12] His response was direct: *"You speak as one of the foolish women speaks,"* and this was something Abraham never had to say for he would have known better than any other person that she was among the *"holy women."* He would have seen this in her walk as she journeyed with him, and heard it in her talk as they conversed. Was she not aware, for instance, that her husband was *"the friend of God"?*[13] Did he not share with her the life-changing and heart-warming assurances that God gave when He asked, *"Shall I hide from Abraham what I am doing?"*[14]

Along with this, we may also ask if God revealed what He would achieve in His purpose through him without telling him about Sarah's connection to it. As the freewoman in Galatians 4:22-5:1, she symbolised the freedom that belongs to the new covenant, which promises every believer liberty in Christ. Is it thinkable that he then would have hidden this from her? Or is it possible that he never shared with her the joy that must have been connected to seeing what the Lord told the Jews in John 8:56, *"Your father Abraham rejoiced to see My day, and he saw it and was glad."* He lived with a holy woman who trusted in God, and through that holiness her confidence and hope were in the Holy One, which would have allowed him confidently to share everything with her. Do you not think it seems most unlikely that God would hide from Sarah what He would do?

Perhaps it is worth noting at this point that the word "holy" – *qādōsh* – is never used to describe anyone in the book of Genesis, although God used its close neighbour in chapter 2:3 when He *"blessed the seventh day, and sanctified* [from *qādash*] *it."* It is one of the wonders of our Bibles that the New Testament sometimes reveals what was never made known in the Old, and Peter's comment about Sarah is one example. Jude's short letter gives other examples of how God moves from former Old Testament revelation to fresh New Testament revelation by current inspiration.[15]

Sarah ... whose daughters you are

As we bow before the glory of a holy God, our hearts readily admit that none of us could take a single step in the spiritual journey He has planned unless, first of all, He had called us to it. This is tremendously clear in the case of Abraham: *"The God of glory appeared unto our father Abraham, when he was in Mesopotamia, before he dwelt in Charran, and said unto him, 'Get thee out of thy country and from thy kindred, and come into the land which I shall shew thee.'"*[16] That call had two distinct parts: 'Get out' and 'come into,' which meant leaving ungodliness and entering into what was of God. And so their journey began, based on a God-centred call from the God of glory, and it continued in the glory of a God-centred walk that focused on the God of holiness. The call of God still occupies this high ground. Yes, it is for man, but it is not man-centred, as much twentieth and twenty-first century preaching has made the gospel appear to be. The call of God still has two main objectives: to bring us out of our sin, and to bring us into His holiness. Its purpose through the cross is to deliver us from our old sinful nature and deliver us to being *"partakers of the divine nature,"*[17] so that we might detest and disown the old and delight in the new.

But what is holiness? It is the intrinsic nature of God, and this is revealed in the things that He does. He is not holy because He does holy things; He does holy things because He is holy. This is as certain a saying that He is not God because He does godly things, but that He does godly things because He is God. In the same way, our personal holiness, our

11

sanctification, comes from being like Him, to be as He is, to think as He thinks, to feel as He feels, and to act as He acts. It is entirely bound up in *being* that it might be expressed in our *doing*: not in the other way around. This is God's order, that our doing will flow out of our being, not that our being will flow out of our doing. In the right order, holy desires will lead to obedience and doing, and our doing will lead on to farther obedience and holy desires.

Naturally, our old nature drives us *to do*; spiritually, our new nature in Christ draws us *to be*, as our newfound hope in Him draws us from the bondage and sinfulness of what we were into the freedom and holiness of who He is. By doing this for us, the claims of the gospel cry out, *"Sin shall not have dominion over you,"*[18] and this is for one great reason: that holiness might have dominion over us. If we borrow the meaning that some have attached to Sarai, then we also have had a name-change that takes us from what had dominion over us into a majestic relationship with the sovereignty of God implied in her new name, Sarah, as princess.

Sin was the dominating force prior to our salvation; and holiness should be the new and ever-current dominating force through our salvation. We say through, and not only after, since our daily salvation that we have to *"work out ... with fear and trembling"*[19] utterly depends on following after holiness.[20] In essence, it is God's nature being embraced in our lives through the inner working of the Holy Spirit and communion with the Holy One who says, *"Be holy, for I am holy."*[21] "I AM" is the eternal and ever-present name of God,[22] *egō eimi* – so often used by the Lord Jesus Christ, and when Peter penned God's words, "I am holy," the phrase *egō hagios eimi* puts His eternal and ever-present holiness at the centre of His name.

Being conscious of our sinfulness will lead to a conscious need for repentance, which only God can give. This is true of the sinner who comes to Christ for salvation[23] and for believers in their restoration to fellowship with Him.[24] In days where so many easy-going attitudes prevail, it would be easy to overlook the need for on-going repentance in our individual experience as Christians and collectively as churches. J.I. Packer puts it well in his book, 'Keep in Step with the Spirit': "Repentance means turning from as much as you know of your sin to give as much as you know of yourself to as much as you know of your God, and as our knowledge grows at these three points so our practice of repentance has to be enlarged." The difficulty is, there will always be conflict within us, personally and inter-personally in our churches, as the holiness of the soul longs for repentance while the old nature resists the desire to confess and become right with God. As far as He is concerned, *"godly sorrow produces repentance,"* which then produces a sevenfold proof of restoration and gives assurance that the offender is now "clear" [from *hagnos*] in the sense that holy [*hagios*] conditions have been restored.

- *diligence* - instead of a careless attitude to sin, they would earnestly follow after righteousness;
- *clearing* - they removed the blight of sinful desire and showed the evidence of having changed;
- *indignation* - rather than finding pleasure in sin, they now show how much it displeased them;
- *fear* - true repentance brings a sense of alarm over how sin undermines righteousness and our reverence for God;
- *vehement desire* - a return to genuine longing for fellowship with God and with one another;
- *zeal* - no longer cold-hearted, but regaining a fervent desire for the holiness of God;
- *vindication* - readiness to put things right with God and with anyone

who has been wronged.

If these vital ingredients of active Christianity depend on repentance in the lives of believers, why is it such an understated part of many churches' ministry? Love for the Word of God, daily commitment to prayer, enjoyment of communion with the Father and His Son, sensitivity to the convicting work of the Holy Spirit, and a healthy desire for Them to produce worship in us, are like pillars in a building. If our reading does not lead ultimately to worship, then we are not reading properly. One reason for this is that we want to read to see what's in it for me rather than by asking, "What's in this for God?" Our tendency is to read, and even study, to find out what God is giving us, but this needs to prompt us to find out what it causes us to give Him. Only by seeing Christ in all the Scriptures will we be able to give something of Christ to God from all the Scripture! All five pillars help to uphold a holy lifestyle. Take them away and we know what happens — the building will collapse.

Repentance stands as a great safeguard to holiness for it is the response of our hearts to the heart of God, which then goes on to condition the thoughts of our minds and the actions of our bodies. If the whole person is not affected, then we may only have been challenged by remorse instead of being changed by repentance. In his book on 'Holiness', J.C. Ryle asks the question: "What is true practical holiness?" – and his answer includes the following:

- Holiness is the habit of being of one mind with God;
- A holy man will follow after purity of heart;
- A holy man will follow after the fear of God;
- A holy man will follow after humility;
- A holy man will follow after faithfulness.

But what is true about a holy man is also true of "holy women," so we can safely conclude that Sarah was a woman whose mind was in tune with God's mind, her heart sought the purity of His heart, she had reverence for Him, humbly followed after Him, and faithfully served Him. Just as she couldn't have been the "freewoman" without living in a personal sense of His freedom, so also she couldn't have been numbered among the "holy women" without a personal sense of His holiness. Paul's point about Abraham still causes us to realise that present-day Christians live by faith and are viewed as his seed;[25] and Peter's point about Sarah still causes us to realise that today's Christian women who live in holiness are viewed as her daughters. What an honour to be numbered among them for, not only are they adorned with godly features, they also honour God by adorning the doctrine of God our Saviour in all things.[26]

Chapter 2 Questions

1. One aspect of Sarah's submissive spirit was that she *"obeyed Abraham, calling him lord."* By contrast, Abigail referred to her husband as *"this scoundrel Nabal. For as his name is, so is he"* (1 Sam.25:25). Does this imply she wasn't submissive?

2. Outline the ways in which you submit to *"the hidden person of the heart"* (1 Pet.3:4) and nurture *"the inward man"* (Rom.7:22) so that you glorify God in your body (1 Cor.6:20; Eph.3:16,17; Col.3:17).

3. Do you ever tend to react like Job's wife when God's will permits something that conflicts with your own will? How do you handle it when you are tempted to think negatively of God? (Rom.8:6,27; 12:2; Heb.10:35,36)

4. How does knowing God (Dan.11:32; 1 Pet.1:16) more intimately and embracing His nature help: a) your desire for personal holiness? b) your consciousness of sin? c) your readiness to ask Him for repentance? d) your experience of 2 Corinthians 7:11?

5. The opportunity to grow in holiness is a blessing and a challenge, so how do we foster the privilege of being of one mind with God, of purity, reverence, humility, and faithfulness?

Chapter 3: Overlooked Women – Part 1

"Then the king of Egypt spoke to the Hebrew midwives, of whom the name of one was Shiphrah and the name of the other Puah; and he said, 'When you do the duties of a midwife for the Hebrew women, and see them on the birthstools, if it is a son, then you shall kill him; but if it is a daughter, then she shall live.' But the midwives feared God, and did not do as the king of Egypt commanded them, but saved the male children alive" (Ex.1:15-17).

It can be surprising how some Bible characters go unnamed, but are not overlooked, while others who are named are overlooked. One outstanding example of the former is found in Matthew 26:13 when a woman poured fragrant oil on Jesus' head, and His response was, *"Assuredly, I say to you, wherever this gospel is preached in the whole world, what this woman has done will be told as a memorial to her."* To this day, she remains unnamed, but not overlooked. By His authority, the Christ-centredness of her action and will are forever associated as being in harmony with the sovereignty of God's will in the ordering of His life on earth. Equally, by the Son's divine assurance, she is forever memorialised in the record of His inspired Word, and further through being *"preached"* – from *kērussō*, meaning by public proclamation – or by being *"told"* – from *laleō*, which can be preaching by conversation.

Some have thought the woman in Matthew 26, also in Mark 14:3-9, to be Mary of John 12:3, though others think differently. One says, "There is much contention among commentators about the transaction mentioned here, and in John 12:3; some supposing them to be different, others to be the same. Some think that the woman mentioned here was Mary, the sister of Lazarus; others Mary Magdalene; but against the former opinion it is argued that it is not likely, had this been Mary the sister of Lazarus, that Matthew and Mark would have suppressed her name. Besides, say they, we should not confound the repast which is mentioned here, with that mentioned by John. This one was made only two days before the Passover, and that one six days before: the one was made at the house of Simon the leper, the other at the house of Lazarus, John 12:1,2. At this, the woman poured the oil on the head of Christ; at the other, Mary anointed Christ's feet with it."[1]

Another writes, "This event in the house of Simon the leper in Bethany is not the same as that which took place in the house of Simon the Pharisee in Luke 7:36-50. Simon was a common name, and the conversation was completely different on the two occasions. Since an alabaster box of ointment had been broken in Luke 7:37-38, this would have encouraged repetition later under appropriate circumstances. Neither do we believe that this is the same event as recorded in John 12:1-9: the conversations were similar but the deeds were different. The supper in John 12 took place just before the Lord rode into Jerusalem in triumph, but that in Matthew 26 took place just before the Passover. In fact, there was often a duplication of similar events (and sometimes triplication). The cleansing of the temple is recorded in John 2 and Matthew 21; the healing of the blind men is found in Luke 18:25 and Matthew 21; there are two storms scenes (Matt.8:24 and 14:24); twice the Lord fed the multitudes

(Matt.14:15-21; 15:32-39); some of the Beatitudes were spoken twice (Matt.5:3-13; Lk.6:20-23). So we need not be surprised that there were two suppers, with similar yet differing happenings at each."[2]

In contrast to an unnamed woman who has been the focus of much gospel preaching, we turn to think of two named women who may seldom have been mentioned in Bible teachers' messages.

Shiphrah and Puah

If we are ever tempted to think that God's description of a woman as being *"the weaker vessel"*[3] is a put-down, we should lay 1 Corinthians 1:27 alongside it. *"But God has chosen ... the weak things of the world to put to shame the things which are mighty."* He never speaks of women as being weak, but only as *"weaker"* than men in the physical sense. What He does say is that all of us are mutually *"weak"* through our humanity and iniquity[4] and that He works through us, spiritually, to manifest His power.

There is a vital connection between the prevention of male deaths in Exodus 12 through the provision of the God-given Passover lamb and the prevention of male deaths in Exodus 1 through the provision of two God-honouring midwives. That connection, of course, is Moses, whose birth often draws preachers' attention to Pharaoh's unnamed daughter, while, at the same time, makes little or no mention of Shiphrah and Puah.

One of the great principles of Scripture that seldom dawns on world rulers is that *"The king's heart is in the hand of the LORD, like the rivers of water; He turns it wherever He wishes."*[5] Two chapters earlier, Solomon expressed the same principle of the sovereignty of God in a different way: *"There are many devices in a man's heart; nevertheless the counsel of the LORD, that shall stand."*[6] Pharaoh was about to learn the hard lesson that God makes the wrath of man to praise Him.[7] Before doing it by death through Moses in the Passover and subsequent destruction in the Red Sea, God did it by birth through these two women who probably represented a company of midwives under their charge. In three overwhelming displays of His wisdom and power, He overcame the feebleness of Pharaoh's schemes in chapter 1 and 2, the firstborn of his sons in chapter 12, and the force of his soldiers in chapter 14.

Thus the tyrant who wanted to slay Israel's sons had his own slain; and then, having planned to have them drowned, saw the might of his own nation drowned in the Red Sea. It's also to God's glory that the daughter of the man who wanted all Hebrew sons killed had compassion on the infant Moses and wanted Jochebed to *"nurse him for me, and I will give you your wages."*[8] The irony is not lost, that 'the glory of Jehovah' – the meaning of Jochebed's name – ensured that Moses survived and was then handed over to be educated in the household that condemned him.

The contrast between the mind of Pharaoh and the mind of God could hardly be more distinct. James summed up the Pharaoh-like mindset: *"This wisdom does not descend from above, but is earthly, sensual, demonic."* He then added, *"But the wisdom that is from above is first pure, then peaceable, gentle, willing to yield, full of mercy and good fruits, without partiality and without hypocrisy."*[9] God wonderfully overcame the wisdom of a brutal tyrant by providing His wisdom through the gentleness of a nurse. Even then, He used the weak things of the world to confound the mighty. Truly, the glory of Jehovah!

Brightness and Brilliance

Before showing His glory through a godly mother and an ungodly daughter, God was glorified in the way these two midwives nerved every midwife among His people. Like Jochebed, they lived up to the meaning of their names. Apart from 'Brightness' and 'Brilliance,' they could be known as 'Glisten' and 'Glitter,' and it's interesting to see how thoughts of Shiphrah's name are woven into Scripture. Job helps us to capture the brightness of God's creation by saying, *"By His Spirit He adorned the heavens,"*[10] or, as translated in the Revised Version, *"the heavens are garnished."* What a beautiful way to speak of the intricate *"work of* [His] *fingers"*[11] – garnishing the skies! And He did it by speaking *"For He spoke, and it was done."*[12] In a similar way, He speaks into our lives and through our lives that we, like Naphtali in Genesis 49:21 (RV), might give *"goodly words"* – words that brighten, words that glisten, words that garnish. The midwives certainly did, and they showed why they did it, and how they did it.

* But the midwives feared God

With the full authority of the Holy Spirit's inspiration lying behind his words in Romans 3:18, the apostle Paul condemns the fallen nature of all mankind by quoting from Psalm 36:1, *"There is no fear of God before their eyes."* David applied it individually, Paul generally, and we can draw two guiding principles from their statements. Unbelievers have no sense of the fear of God and their desires, behaviour and lifestyle prove that they don't. Believers should have a sense of the fear of God, and their desires, behaviour and lifestyle should prove that they do. Why then is the former glaringly obvious, and the latter not?

The reason for the first is, *"There is none righteous, no, not one; there is none who understands; there is none who seeks after God. They have all turned aside; they have together become unprofitable; there is none who does good, no, not one.*"[13] Our whole world is deeply tainted by the absence of reverence for God. Many believe He doesn't exist, therefore no need to revere a non-existent Person. Some believe there could be a God, but not One in whom they personally should be interested or who is personally interested in them. Between these two dismissive declarations, millions believe what they like, think what they like, and do what they like, while ungodly social laws accommodate sin and violate holiness.

The reason for the second is, that we don't live with a big enough sense of God or an acute enough sense of sin. These are serious considerations for everyone in the book of Exodus. Pharaoh resisted the fear of the LORD God in chapter 9:30; leaders were required to fear God in 18:21 if their ability and integrity were to be of any value; and the people must resign themselves to the fear of God in 20:20 if they were to renounce sin. Moses' clarion call to them comes down the centuries to us, *"That His fear may be before you, so that you may not sin."* Of these, it is still essential that leadership among the people of God is not devalued or rendered ineffective due to lack of reverence; His people also are not compromised by treating sin lightly through lack of reverence. God is to be revered and feared: first in relation to His holiness, and then in the matter of judgment, so that our conduct will be governed by a deepening sense of Himself.

If Daniel 11:32 is true, that *"the people who know their God shall be strong, and carry out great exploits,"* then it must be equally true that the people who do not know their God will be weak. Christians and churches need to devote themselves to prayerful consideration of His attributes and nature. The Lord Jesus Christ has urged us, *"Take My yoke upon you and learn from Me,"*[14] and the more we do this the more we will reverence

Him. One thing is sure, a limited sense of God's holiness and greatness will lead to a limited sense of reverence.

Shiphrah and Puah had a decision to make: obey the king or God. But their decision didn't rest on their obedience; it depended on their reverence. From the present-day Christian's point of view, we don't become reverent by being obedient, we become obedient by being reverent. Paul urges us to make it our goal, *"perfecting holiness in the fear of God,"*[15] and this is possible only by reverencing God for who and what He is. Seeing holiness in Him produces reverence in us, and reverence for Him produces holiness in us. With this in mind, the writer of Hebrews 12:14 encourages us to *"Pursue peace with all people, and holiness, without which no one will see the Lord."* Having the peace of God allows us to pursue peace and communion with others; and having the holiness of God allows us to pursue sanctification before others. By living in the reality of both, we will live in the expectation of seeing Him while, at the same time, help others to see Him in us. James 1:4 (ESV) gives this guiding principle: *"Let steadfastness have its full effect, that you may be perfect and complete, lacking in nothing."* May it be so in us for His Name's sake.

* Did not do as the king commanded

These women had the order right: they feared God rather than the enemy, and they obeyed God rather than the enemy. They are great examples to us all for they preferred to let holiness produce God-honouring service rather than let temptation produce man-pleasing sin. This meant that God received the pleasure of their faith rather than man relishing the pleasure of their fall. They leave each of us with a very important decision to make each time we are tempted: either we let reverence keep us from sin or we let sin keep us from reverence. This was their number one reason for not sinning for they *"feared God, and did not do."* For them, doing was not optional, nor would it have been confidential for their mission would soon have been discovered; but it wasn't the fear of being found out that kept them from sin, nor should it be with us. Being transparent with God calls for honesty and integrity before others.

* Saved the male children alive

This was consistent with their calling as midwives. It was the whole object of their service to see a mother through to the eventual joy of childbirth, and their only hope of job-satisfaction. More than that, it was their God-honouring obligation among His people to assist the growth of the infant nation, and failure to fulfil His purpose would have been an extremely serious matter. The call of God and the purpose of God remain the highest reasons for what we want to do, similarly for what we don't want to do. These dear women had the expansion of God's people at heart, and so must we. Our mandate is no less that Paul's in Philippians 1:27 and 28 – *"Only let your conduct be worthy of the gospel of Christ, so that whether I come and see you or am absent, I may hear of your affairs, that you stand fast in one spirit, with one mind striving together for the faith of the gospel, and not in any way terrified by your adversaries, which is to them a proof of perdition, but to you of salvation, and that from God."*

Some have asked why the midwives sought to placate Pharaoh when he asked, *"Why **have you done** this?"* but that would be the wrong question. Pharaoh's was that of an unregenerate man. As believers, ours must focus on the God-glorifying reason why they *"**did not do** as the king of Egypt commanded them."* It would have meant little to him had they replied that they *"feared God,"* but it means a lot to us as we endeavour to learn from their faithfulness. Under the convicting power of the Holy Spirit, the voice of conscience may be clear in saying why wrong reasoning allowed us to commit a particular sin, but is it equally clear in giving the right reason for why we didn't? Our only reason for resisting sin is the same as for pursuing holiness: it is reverence for God.

Every place of work is a place of testimony. Every employer will have expectations, some of which may have questionable work ethics. Every Christian employee has a decision to make at such times, and it may be that you cannot comply because of your reverence for God. However, you may not be readily understood if your answer is, "I feared God," but, knowing this is your reason, you will be able to explain it in a way that is. Irrespective of our job, our own work ethic must be governed by reverence for Him: *"Whatever you do, work heartily, as for the Lord and not for men, knowing that from the Lord you will receive the inheritance as your reward. You are serving the Lord Christ."*[16] When asked to pass on an untrue message for his boss, a Christian said he wasn't able to do it. When asked, "Why?" the Christian replied, "I couldn't lie for you, and for the same reason I wouldn't lie to you."

* God dealt well with the midwives

As verse 17 ran its course time-wise between the two appearings of the women before Pharaoh in verses 16 and 18, God watched over their work and took pleasure in it. His response could be summed up, as it was toward Gentile believers in Acts 15:8: *"So God, who knows the heart, acknowledged them,"* and He *"dealt well with the midwives."* They had done well, and He could have told them *"that it may go well with you and your children after you, when you do what is right in the sight of the LORD."*[17] The thought of dealing with them comes from the word *yātab* with its thought of acceptance, as in God's challenge to Cain: *"If you do well, will you not be accepted?"*[18] It also means they found favour, but there's a lovely application in Exodus 30:7, which draws from the same word and speaks of Aaron when he *"tends the lamps."* This was done to maintain the brightness of the lampstand in the holy place of the tabernacle, but long before Aaron was privileged to do this in chapter 30 God tended Shiphrah and Puah in their Brightness and Brilliance. They had such confidence in Him, and there could hardly be more resounding voices than theirs in Scripture to urge us, as the writer to Hebrews does in chapter 10:35, *"Therefore do not cast away your confidence, which has great reward."*

* He provided households for them

With many others being blessed in an early expression of Psalm 127:3 – *"Behold, children are a heritage from the LORD, the fruit of the womb is a reward"* – God then rewarded both midwives and gave them early proof that *"He is a rewarder of those who diligently seek Him."*[19] In connection with this, Keil and Delitzsch say in their commentary, "God rewarded them for their conduct, Through not carrying out the ruthless command of the king, they had helped to build up the families of Israel, and their own families were therefore built up by God." As the book of Exodus opened, God knew how critical these two women were to the progress and unfolding of His purpose, and it would be good for us to keep this at the forefront of our minds as we read its pages. The whole book in its revelation of God, together with the gathering of the twelve tribes in their place of service owes much to these unsung heroines of chapter 1.

Chapter 3 Questions

1. How can we nurture a deepening sense of God in our lives personally and collectively in the churches? Are there ways in which our own daily reading could be combined with more systematic teaching in church gatherings?
2. In what sort of ways can reverence for God and a keener sense of the fear of God be fostered in our daily walk as Christians and, once again, how can churches focus more on this aspect of discipleship?
3. Suggest ways in which the principle of Exodus 1:17 – *"They feared God and did not do"* – can be effectively applied in our temptations and decision making.
4. These women fulfilled their calling by seeing it as part of honouring God's purpose in the growth and service of His people. How do scriptures such as Romans 8:28 and 2 Timothy 1:9 help us to do the same?
5. Shiphrah and Puah didn't lose their brightness and God rewarded them in a way that resembled how Aaron would *"tend the lamps"* (Ex.30:7). Are there ways in which Christ, as our great High Priest, maintains the light of our testimony?

Chapter 4: Overlooked Women – Part 2

"Then came the daughters of Zelophehad the son of Hepher, the son of Gilead, the son of Machir, the son of Manasseh, from the families of Manasseh the son of Joseph; and these were the names of his daughters: Mahlah, Noah, Hoglah, Milcah, and Tirzah. And they stood before Moses, before Eleazar the priest, and before the leaders and all the congregation, by the doorway of the tabernacle of meeting, saying: 'Our father died in the wilderness; but he was not in the company of those who gathered together against the LORD, in company with Korah, but he died in his own sin; and he had no sons. Why should the name of our father be removed from among his family because he had no son? Give us a possession among our father's brothers.' So Moses brought their case before the LORD. And the LORD spoke to Moses, saying: "The daughters of Zelophehad speak what is right; you shall surely give them a possession of inheritance among their father's brothers, and cause the inheritance of their father to pass to them" (Numbers 27:1–7).

N othing compares with the satisfaction of knowing that God has spoken. Nor is there anything like the sense of peace and justice that He gives in times when difficulties seem to be insurmountable. The main problem for these women was that there was no precedent in law that could provide the answer they longed for.

It's a very public scene that is before us in Numbers 27, but it speaks volumes in regard to what must have taken place in the privacy of their own home. Nothing is said about it, but we can deduce from everything they said publicly that their private discussions were of a carefully considered and God-honouring nature. Had they gone wrong there, nothing could have been right afterward, neither would God have been able to say, *"The daughters of Zelophehad speak what is right."* His commendation lets us conclude that they were "right" with Him in the end, because they had been "right" with Him from the beginning. We will see this as we review the steps they took together to prevent anything from going wrong.

Their approach to Moses and leaders before the people

If ever there was an early proof of *"your Father who sees in secret will reward you openly,"*[1] this was it. It was time spent secretly with Him that allowed them to stand openly before Moses the mediator, Eleazar the high priest, the leaders, and all the people at the door of the tabernacle, which meant, most importantly, standing before God. This was no Old Testament example of a militant women's rights movement or activists making an unruly demand. Rather it was a quiet work of God in the hearts of five bereaved sisters that spread just as quietly through the hearts and minds of leadership until it gripped the hearts and minds of the holy nation. In such a spirit of unity, not of protest, they stood as one to seek the mind of God. Nor was there any trace of a hasty spirit making impatient demands on Him. This was 'women of worth' waiting by faith and for as long as it would take, uniting their burden from their dwelling place with the anticipation of blessing from Him in His dwelling place.

They would never have thought that God would set their experience in His Word to teach us how to turn issues around that have the ability to divide until they show their ability to unite. It was orderliness at its best, and we can't help but see a marked contrast with the disorderliness of previous chapters. It was as if God were saying, *"If My people who are called by My name will humble themselves, and pray and seek My face, and turn from their wicked ways, then I will hear from heaven, and will forgive their sin and heal their land. Now My eyes will be open and My ears attentive to prayer made in this place."*[2]

Their measured response to their father's death

Grief can cause irrational thoughts to take root, and these can lead to detrimental actions, but neither of these was true of those five sisters. Long before Solomon penned his proverbs, they lived by the principle, *"Commit your works to the LORD, and your thoughts will be established."*[3] They also knew that ordered thoughts lead to ordered ways, and we could adapt David's words in Psalm 37:23 and apply them to all five – *"The steps of a good* [woman] *are ordered by the LORD, and He delights in* [her] *way."* Solomon thought of this process being like a set of scales as he wrote, *"Make level the path of thy feet, and let all thy ways be ordered aright."*[4] It's part of the learning curve of our lives that we allow God to weigh our spirits,[5] our hearts,[6] and our actions.[7]

Deciding to take their burden to Moses and to God was the calculation of their godly and stable character, and we know this from their acceptance; not so much of how, but of why their father died. Although they knew he had not been caught up in the rebellion against Moses and Aaron in Numbers 16, they submitted to what was true about many others, *"he died in his own sin."* Whatever it was, God knew, and they accepted that he was part of His earlier pronouncement in chapter 14:29 and 30:

> *"The carcasses of you who have complained against Me shall fall in this wilderness, all of you who were numbered, according to your entire number, from twenty years old and above, except for Caleb the son of Jephunneh and Joshua the son of Nun, you shall by no means enter the land which I swore I would make you dwell in."*

It's very noticeable that the closing words of chapter 26 were the fulfilment of this, and it's equally noticeable that the next words are, *"Then came the daughters of Zelophehad."* They were at the very heart of God's timing! The reality that fulfilled judgment had included their father was unavoidable, nevertheless, they seemed to claim God's promise in chapter 14:31, *"But your little ones ... I will bring in, and they shall know the land which you have despised."* There are two things here that hold sterling lessons. First is, that we need to be at our most stable if, or when, a family member or friend comes under the judgement of God. These women never wavered under the influence of harbouring thoughts of injustice, nor did they react in the flesh by becoming argumentative. The second is, God had said they would *"know the land,"* and they wanted to *"know"* it in as real and rich and meaningful way as possible. To them, this meant they didn't want to be there as mere spectators. They wanted actively to be involved and enter into *"the good of the land, and leave it as an inheritance to* [their] *children forever."*[8] The problem was, their father's death precluded them from enjoying his inheritance, since he had no sons to whom it could be passed on.

Their reasoning regarding inheritance law

In the absence of a law that would grant daughters entitlement, and the apparent unfairness that excluded them, they presented their case. There was nothing unreasonable or hot-headed in their approach. They had only one question: *"Why should the name of our father be removed from among his family because he had no son?"* We can only assume that the urgency of the matter, coupled with the fervency of the sisters, caused Moses' immediate response – *"So Moses brought their case before the LORD."*

Their appeal for justice

With their reasoning resting on one question, their accompanying appeal was based on a simple statement: *"Give us a possession among our father's brothers."* It was the voicing of a yearning that may have escaped some young men among the people of God for whom it was enough to be there with their father. These women wanted to hold on to something in the land, something they could call their own, and possess it with a real sense of belonging. The word *"chuzzāh* comes from *'āchaz,* which showed they wanted a strong attachment to the land, as if they were fastened to it. The word revealed the strength of its bond in 2 Chronicles 9:17 and 18 when Solomon *"... made a great throne of ivory, and overlaid it with pure gold. The throne had six steps, with a footstool of gold, which were fastened to the throne ..."* There is no escaping the thought that the steps were at one with the throne, to the extent that the throne possessed the steps and the steps possessed the throne. That was what these sisters were looking for in the land: the land was in their hearts, and they wanted their hearts to be in the land. Nothing more; nothing less!

It is ever God's desire that His people *"possess their possessions,"*[9] both by enjoying them and by protecting them. Solomon's warning in Proverbs 10:4 was true long before he wrote it: *"He who has a slack hand becomes poor."* For this reason, God's people lost their grip on what he had given and, by treating divine things so lightly, were taken into captivity in Babylon. Before this, such as in the days of Jehoshaphat, their enemies tried to dispossess them, and he concluded that they were *"coming to throw us out of Your possession which You have given us to inherit."*[10] Their aim was, *"Let us take for ourselves the pastures of God for a possession."*[11] What a lovely phrase, "the pastures of God"! Oh, that we might treat God's things as they truly are! Some versions of Scripture say "houses" instead of "pastures," but the word n^e'ōt from nā'āh allows both. For instance, the King James Version says "houses" in Psalm 83:12, while all major versions say "pastures" in Psalm 23:2. Houses are where people feel at home, and spiritually speaking God's people should feel at home in possessing our possessions. Pastures are figurative of where they feed. Put them together, and they should have heightened their appreciation and caused them to inherit their inheritance.

God graciously delivered His people from captivity in Babylon, and will deliver them again when the Lord comes to redeem them at the end of the great tribulation. God's promise to Israel in Isaiah 59:20 is, *"The Redeemer will come to Zion, and to those who turn from transgression in Jacob."* In that day, Obadiah's words will be truer than ever: *"But on Mount Zion there shall be deliverance, and there shall be holiness; the house of Jacob shall possess their possessions."* Deliverance, holiness, possessions: by the goodness of God, one leads to the other. Deliverance causes those who are delivered to hold their God-given possessions, and holiness allows them to hold them in the way they should be held. In the presence of their once rejected, but risen and returned Messiah, Israel at last will inherit her inheritance.

God's response

From the flow of verse 1-11 in Number 27, it would seem there was no delay between the daughters coming to Moses, in Moses coming to God, in God's fourfold response, and in Moses speaking to the people and to the five women.

- *"The daughters of Zelophehad speak what is right;*
- *You shall surely give them a possession of inheritance among their father's brothers, and cause his inheritance to pass to them;*
- *And you shall speak to the children of Israel, saying: 'If a man dies and has no son, then you shall cause his inheritance to pass to his daughter';*
- *And it shall be to the children of Israel a statute of judgment."*

Israel saw history being made that day, yet nothing is recorded of the daughters' delight or of the people's recognition of what these sisters had championed. Instead, just as Aaron had been replaced by Eleazar in chapter 20, God told Moses to *"Go up into this Mount Abarim, and see the land ... And when you have seen it, you also shall be gathered to your people, as Aaron your brother was gathered."* Five women went home assured of their inheritance; Moses saw the land from afar, but didn't enter into the inheritance; and Joshua was commissioned to lead the people into theirs. Well might we join in singing *"the song of Moses, the servant of God, and the song of the Lamb, saying, "Great and marvellous are your deeds, O Lord God the Almighty! Just and true are your ways, O King of the nations!"*[12]

A Word for Today

From the moment of trusting in the Lord Jesus Christ as Saviour, believers are exposed to the unsearchable riches of Christ that God makes known through *"the riches of His goodness,"*[13] *"the riches of His glory,"*[14] and *"the riches of His grace."*[15] Were these only for the enriching of a lifelong relationship with Him, for the deepening of our understanding of Him, and for the growth of our likeness to Him, we would be well-blessed. Wonderful as this is, it stops short of what God has in store in what He calls *"the promise of the eternal inheritance."*[16] This verse points to three major thoughts that ought to become the consuming interest of every believer in appreciation of our Saviour's death: a greater Mediator than Moses, a better covenant than the old, and an eternal inheritance rather than a temporal.

* Our inheritance in salvation – Acts 26:18

The gift of God is eternal life,[17] and with it comes the assurance of an eternal inheritance. This is the third time the writer to the Hebrews attaches the word "eternal" in chapter 9, having already spoken of our *"eternal salvation"* in 5:9. He speaks of *"eternal redemption"* in verse 12, *"the eternal Spirit"* in verse 14, and now *"the eternal inheritance"* in verse 15, and he links all of them with Christ's suffering and death. In a similar way, Romans 8 presents the essential nature of Jesus' death before leading on to emphasise *"and if children, then heirs – heirs of God and joint heirs with Christ"* in verse 16. Just as we rejoice in being saved and relating our salvation to Him as Saviour, so we also rejoice that being heirs causes us to relate our inheritance to Him as Heir.

Again, the writer of Hebrews exalts Him in chapter 1:2 as *"heir of all things,"* but he is careful to point out that this was by God's appointment.

35

More than a thousand years earlier, God spoke of this through David in Psalm 2:6 and 7: *"Yet I have set My King on My holy hill of Zion." "I will declare the decree: The LORD has said to Me, 'You are My Son, today I have begotten You. Ask of Me, and I will give You the nations for Your inheritance, and the ends of the earth for Your possession.'"* Both Old and New Testament combine to laud *"the eternal purpose which He* [God] *accomplished in Christ Jesus."*[18]

This helps us to understand why the Lord told the parable of the wicked vinedressers in Matthew 21:33-46. Their brutal killing of the landowner's son was a reflection of Israel's treatment of the Messiah, as captured in their evil statement, *"This is the heir. Come let us kill him and seize his inheritance."* In applying this to the Lord, God allowed them to kill His Son, but never let them seize the inheritance of the Heir. They could do the first part, because it was essential to the eternal purpose; but they couldn't do the second part, because it wasn't in the sovereign will of Him who says, *"Surely, as I have thought, so it shall come to pass, and as I have purposed, so it shall stand."*[19]

Having finished the work that His Father gave Him to do on the cross,[20] He then went home to glory that He might apply that finished work to the lives of repentant sinners – *"to open their eyes, in order to turn them from darkness to light, and from the power of Satan to God, that they may receive forgiveness of sins and an inheritance among those who are sanctified by faith in Me."* What a change: and all because Jesus is Light, God, Redeemer, and Heir! In that change, we continue to walk by the help of the Holy Spirit *"who is the guarantee of our inheritance until the redemption of the purchased possession, to the praise of His glory."*[21] Neither it nor we can be lost!

* Our inheritance in Scripture – Acts 20:32

The Word of God is the means by which every believer is led to Christ. It's the way God begins with everyone who comes to faith, since *"Faith comes by hearing, and hearing by the word of God."*[22] It's also the way He continues to speak into our lives: to teach, to guide, to feed, and to strengthen. It's vital then that, to be among the 'Women God Moved' and the 'Men God Moved,' we must be moved by His Word. For this very reason, after Paul had spoken to the elders from the church in Ephesus about facing the danger of wolves savaging the flock, he pointed to God's great safeguarding provision: *"I commend you to God and to the word of His grace, which is able to build you up and give you an inheritance among all those who are sanctified."* As we hear this means of grace being passed on to us, we need to ask, "How much am I drawing from my present inheritance in the Word? Is it leading me? Is it feeding me? Is it edifying me? If not, then I am not spending enough time in it; and the less I am in it, the less it will be in me!

* Our inheritance in service – Gal.5:19-21; Eph.5:1-5

In our last chapter, the midwives in Egypt taught us a fundamental lesson: only the fear of God will keep us from sin. They *"feared God, and did not do."* Struggles against sin are an unavoidable part of human nature and temptation will always be with us while we are in our earthly bodies. Doctor Strong tells us in his concordance that the daughters of Zelophehad had a grandfather, Hepher, whose name meant "a pit of shame." Why he was given this name, we have no idea, but we do know that our fallen, sinful nature causes us to borrow David's words: *"He also brought me up out of a horrible pit, out of the miry clay, and set my feet upon a rock, and established my steps. He has put a new song in my mouth—praise to our God; many will see it and fear, and will trust in the*

LORD."[23]

Like early Christians in the early churches, we are urged to *"put to death the deeds of the body,"*[24] but how do we do it? How do we overcome? Similar questions needed to be asked regarding problems in the churches of Galatia and Ephesus, and they needed to know that the answers don't lie in ecclesiology but in Christology. Paul's answer to the Galatians was, *"Walk in the Spirit, and you shall not fulfil the lust of the flesh."*[25] To the Ephesians it was fourfold:

1. "Walk *worthy of the calling"* (4:1)
2. *"Walk in love."* (5:2)
3. *"Walk as children of light"* (5:8) and
4. *"Walk circumspectly"* (5:15).

The whole matter of walking consistently with the rule of God belongs to *"how you ought to walk and to please God."*[26] This means that, just as the grace of God affects how we *"stand"*[27] before Him, it also should affect how we *"walk."* It means walking in a way that is compatible with the inheritance that takes character from our calling from sin to God, from enmity to love, from darkness to light, and from folly to wisdom. A greater sense of the lordship of Christ in our salvation coupled with a greater sense of His lordship in His Word would give us a greater sense of His lordship in our walk. We can do no better than employ Paul's mandate in Colossians 2:6 and 7 – *"As you have therefore received Christ Jesus the Lord, so walk in Him, rooted and built up in Him and established in the faith, as you have been taught, abounding in it with thanksgiving."* This unites the inheritance of our salvation with our inheritance in the Word and gives us the power to walk acceptably in the inheritance of our service.

Chapter 4 Questions

1. When something seems uncertain in your church, as it did in Numbers 27, how do you make sure that discussions in the home are of "a carefully considered and God-honouring nature?" How would you apply *"a more excellent way"* (1 Cor.12:31)?

2. In what sort of ways can the daughters' orderly approach *"before Moses, before Eleazar the priest, and before the leaders and all the congregation, by the doorway of the tabernacle"* be used as a guide to solving matters in present-day church life?

3. God has made it wonderfully possible for disciples of the Lord Jesus Christ to enjoy all three aspects of our spiritual inheritance. In what ways are you enjoying: a) *"The promise of the eternal inheritance"* in your salvation (Heb.9:15)? b) Our inheritance in the Scriptures (Acts 20:32)? c) Our inheritance in service (Gal.5:16-21; Eph.5:1-17)?

Chapter 5: Deborah

"When Ehud was dead, the children of Israel again did evil in the sight of the LORD. So the LORD sold them into the hand of Jabin king of Canaan, who reigned in Hazor. The commander of his army was Sisera, who dwelt in Harosheth Hagoyim. And the children of Israel cried out to the LORD; for Jabin had nine hundred chariots of iron, and for twenty years he had harshly oppressed the children of Israel. Now Deborah, a prophetess, the wife of Lapidoth, was judging Israel at that time. And she would sit under the palm tree of Deborah between Ramah and Bethel in the mountains of Ephraim. And the children of Israel came up to her for judgment.

"Then she sent and called for Barak the son of Abinoam from Kedesh in Naphtali, and said to him, 'Has not the LORD God of Israel commanded, "Go and deploy troops at Mount Tabor; take with you ten thousand men of the sons of Naphtali and of the sons of Zebulun; and against you I will deploy Sisera, the commander of Jabin's army, with his chariots and his multitude at the River Kishon; and I will deliver him into your hand"?' And Barak said to her, 'If you will go with me, then I will go; but if you will not go with me, I will not go!' So she said, 'I will surely go with

you; nevertheless there will be no glory for you in the journey
you are taking, for the LORD will sell Sisera into the hand of a
woman.' Then Deborah arose and went with Barak to Kedesh"
(Judg.4:1-9).

S piritual landslides were common in Israel. They happened in
the change-over from one king to another, and they happened
between judges. Irrespective of long years of triumph under
good spiritual leadership, the people of God had a remarkable ability
not to share or retain their spirituality or their vision. Their overruling
weakness was that *"they would not listen to their judges,"* even though
"the LORD was with the judge and delivered them out of the hand of their
enemies all the days of the judge."[1] True to form, they groaned under
enemy oppression, yet deliverance known through judges didn't keep
them from going back to it. Forty years of rest under 'the force of God'
through Othniel didn't keep them back, neither did eighty years under
Ehud, or the combined forty years under Tola and Jair.[2] At first, the
enemy was from far off Mesopotamia, then it was much closer from
Moab; but following the death of Ehud, it was closer still, right on their
own doorstep within the land of Canaan.[3] Othniel "prevailed" over the
first, Ehud "subdued" the second, but what would it take to vanquish
the third? The answer was, a woman.

No reference is made to her parentage, though they undoubtedly chose
her name; and no mention is made of her husband, other than that
she was the wife of Lapidoth. His name means a lamp or a torch, but
evidently not ready to shine as she did, otherwise God could have used
him. There was one man to whom she did turn, Barak, whose name
meant lightning, yet his response was hardly as quick: more like a long-
awaited rumble of thunder after a lightning flash that indicates the
response was miles off! When called by her to lead ten thousand men

into battle at the command of God, his conditional response was, *"If you will go with me, then I will go; but if you will not go with me, I will not go!"*[4] So she had two men: one like a lamp at home; the other, like lightning on the battlefield, yet she was brighter than both! Perhaps, Barak wanted the assurance of her prophetic presence in the heat of the battle, and not have to ask, like Jehoshaphat, *"Is there not a prophet of the LORD here whom we might inquire of him?"*[5]

Alternatively, he may have been like Deborah's successor, Gideon, to whom God said, *"But if you are afraid to go down, go down to the camp with Purah your servant."*[6] In the goodness of God, fears and failures can be great teachers in the school of faith, and the trajectory of its learning curve can lead us upward until we say, *"Behold, God is my salvation, I will trust and not be afraid."*[7] Nothing makes this clearer than the thirty-second verse of Hebrews 11, *"And what more shall I say? For the time would fail me to tell of Gideon and Barak and Samson and Jephthah."* These four men are listed in this great gallery of faith and, like others in the chapter, they overcame faults to live by faith, including Barak whose faith was stirred by a godly woman.

A mother in Israel

Mothers are as necessary as fathers. This is true, both naturally and spiritually. Job was a man with a wide-ranging ministry, and he knew how to make it available at *"the gate of the city,"*[8] whereas Deborah chose to *"sit under the palm tree of Deborah between Ramah and Bethel in the mountains of Ephraim."* Even figuratively, this was a strategic position, as she made herself available and accessible on the heights, near to the house of God, and in the region named after fruitfulness. Two aspects of her identity help us to see that she had no intention of usurping a man's role among the people of God, yet she was conscious that His call in her life was to be fulfilled outside of her home not only as *"the wife of Lapidoth"* on the battlefield, but as *"a mother in Israel."*[9]

It's equally true that motherliness is as necessary as fatherliness. Long before Paul told the Corinthians, *"You do not have many fathers,"*[10] God showed His people the fatherliness of their Father, and confirmed its abiding truth in new covenant language in Jeremiah 31:9, *"I am a Father to Israel."* He also assures them through Isaiah 66:13, *"As one whom his mother comforts, so I will comfort you,"* and this shows us that Job and Deborah both drew from the nature of God to fulfil their ministries. Jamieson, Fausset and Brown put it this way in their commentary, "Deborah assumed the office of ruler and counsellor, not for the gratification of her personal ambition, but for the good of the people over whom she watched with the lively interest and solicitude of a mother over her children."

To this, we can add the thought given by Keil and Delitzsch, "Deborah describes herself as 'a mother in Israel,' on account of her having watched over her people with maternal care, just as Job calls himself a father to the poor who had been supported by him (Job 29:16; cf. Isa.22:21)." So it is evident that, in her motherliness, she drew on the character of God, but she also drew courage from Him as the LORD of Psalm 24: who is *"mighty in battle,"* and through her He would bring renewed faith and triumph to birth.

There is a valuable parallel to this in Paul's letter to the Galatians, as he draws the precious distinction between two covenants, two sons, two women, two mountains – by inference and by linking Hebrews 12:22, *"But you have come to Mount Zion"* – and two cities. These are, the old covenant under law and the new covenant under grace; Ishmael and Isaac; Hagar the bondwoman and Sarah the freewoman; Mount Sinai and Mount Zion; Jerusalem on earth and Jerusalem above. As present-day believers in Christ, we rejoice in the freedom that is from above, granted to us in the miracle of the new birth.

This was the Lord's message to Nicodemus in John 3:7, *"You must be born again."* The word for "again" is *anōthen*, which can be translated as "from above," as in John 19:11 where Jesus said to Pilate, *"You could have no power at all against Me unless it had been given you from above."* The same word is used in James 1:17, *"Every good gift and every perfect gift is from above, and comes down from the Father of lights."* He is the Person from whom we receive this freedom in the new birth, and the Jerusalem that is in heaven is the place from which we get it, therefore it is *"the mother of us all."* We take our character from them, and we also take courage.

Play the men

The King James Version translates Joab's words in 2 Samuel 10:12 as, *"Be of good courage, and let us play the men for our people."* David also encouraged Solomon to *"Be strong, therefore, and prove yourself a man."*[11] He might as well have said, "If you want to be kingly, be manly," for it's not possible to be a man of God without being manly. Twice in Judges 3, *"God raised up a deliverer,"* and both Othniel and Ehud filled His purpose, but there is no indication in chapter 4 that one was available. It was a poor reflection on Israel in Deborah's day that manliness was in such short supply, and they should have been shamed into confession before God in readiness for action for God. Even Barak held back from the call of God, yet there was one thing in his favour: his pedigree. He was *"the son of Abinoam from Kedesh in Naphtali."*[12] If he lived up to his name he would have borne the agreeable character of his father, as a son who wrestled in the refuge of a holy place, and appeared like a flash of light.[13]

Thank God for men and women who strive in prayer, wrestling against the forces of evil while depending on the power of God to overcome. Deborah was aware of divine intervention and acknowledged, *"They fought from the heavens."*[14] How well she knew that supernatural power lay behind the conflict on an earthly battlefield! Paul agrees, and reminds us in Ephesian 6:10-18:

> *"Finally, my brethren, be strong in the Lord and in the power of His might. Put on the whole armor of God, that you may be able to stand against the wiles of the devil. For we do not wrestle against flesh and blood, but against principalities, against powers, against the rulers of the darkness of this age, against spiritual hosts of wickedness in the heavenly places. Therefore take up the whole armor of God, that you may be able to withstand in the evil day, and having done all, to stand.*
>
> *Stand therefore, having girded your waist with truth, having put on the breastplate of righteousness, and having shod your feet with the preparation of the gospel of peace; above all, taking the shield of faith with which you will be able to quench all the fiery darts of the wicked one. And take the helmet of salvation, and the sword of the Spirit, which is the word of God; praying always with all prayer and supplication in the Spirit, being watchful to this end with all perseverance and supplication for all the saints."*

How significant this portion of Scripture is, for it begins with what is *"of God"* and ends with the wearers of that armour being before God *"praying always with all prayer."* Our battles need to be won above before we can win them below! How vital it is that we understand this! We need genuinely to discover that *"A glorious throne set on high from the beginning is the place of our sanctuary,"*[15] and that, if we don't win our battles there in heaven, we won't win them here on earth. Every one of us needs our own personal Kedesh where we grow in holiness. If Barak really knew this sort of separation, then he had learned the secret that true separation leads to sanctification. By contrast, as verse 11 points out, Heber *"had separated himself from the Kenites,"* but it was for selfish reasons and not spiritual. So it is good for us to learn that separation has sanctification at its heart. If not, we will prove that separation without love is legalism; without light, it is dogmatism; and, without life, it is formalism. The danger is, that we shape a habit instead of holiness.

Among David's army in 1 Chronicles 12, verse 32 tells us that the sons of Issachar *"had understanding of the times, to know what Israel ought to do."* Some suggest they read the stars, but it's much more relevant that, in days of uncertainty and confusion, God gave men who knew His will for His people, just as they knew they should recognise David as God's rightful king. In a different context, Paul looked for maturity among those in the church in Corinth, pleading, *"in understanding be men."*[16]

Why is it, then, that we still face similar challenges in our day? Should sisters, who accept their silent roles in a church's worship and prayer and not try to copy their brethren's participation, be left wondering why some brethren imitate their silence rather than enjoy the privilege of speaking with God? May Joab's words come back to urge us to *"play the men for our people."* And David's, too: *"Be strong, therefore, and prove yourself a man."*

No other mind

It is in this freedom we face our battles as those who have overcome the limitations of the law through the perfect sacrifice of our Lord Jesus Christ,[17] and we cannot go back to be held in its bondage. Glorious victory! As Paul continued his reasoning in Galatians chapter 5:13 (ESV) *"For you were called to freedom,"* he had just thought in verse 10 of how they were called to be of *"no other mind"* before launching into how we should treat one another, and how we should conquer fleshly thoughts and actions. The range of hostile intent is intense, and Paul's conclusion in verse 24 is clear-cut: *"Those who are Christ's have crucified the flesh with its passions and desires."* In essence, this is our answer to Deborah's situation.

She knew how great a threat Jabin was to God's people, and would be well aware that his predecessor of the same name had been completely overthrown in Joshua 11. On that occasion, the enemies' chariots were made of wood, which Joshua burned. This time, however, a successor arose with resurgent forces encased in nine hundred chariots of iron, and the same ungodly intentions and cunning. Like his forebears, his name meant 'intelligence,' and it was his captain Sisera's job to implement the mind of his king, on the battlefield. With a carnal mindset in all its hostility to God and hatred for what is of God,[18] Sisera bore testimony to the enmity between Satan and the woman that resulted from Eden's Fall and, ultimately, would focus on *"her Seed"* who would bruise Satan's head as Satan bruised His heel.[19]

Deborah would seem puny opposition against him, but it has been said that with a name, "which signifies a bee," she had "honey for her friends, and a sting for the enemies of Israel" (Practical Truths From Judges by Luke H. Wiseman). Another commentator has said of her name, "Deborah and Debir are practically the same word, and both signify 'the word.'" What a suited instrument for the overthrow of mere human reason" (Lectures on the Book of Judges by Samuel Ridout). She certainly treasured the word of the Lord, and proved it in her opening challenge to Barak, *"Has not the LORD God of Israel commanded."* As a willing servant in the hand of her great God, she is a foreshadowing of the One God calls *"My Servant,"*[20] the Seed of the woman, and *"the Word"*[21] who Himself calls us by *"the word of the cross."*[22]

Having been called into battle, Barak went forward knowing, *"There will be no glory for you in the journey you are taking, for the LORD will sell Sisera into the hand of a woman."* Barak may have thought she meant that God would use her, but she knew differently. The God of whom David would write, *"God has spoken once, twice I have heard this: that power belongs to God,"*[23] had a double message through two women in a day when men were reluctant, if not unable, to rise to the occasion.

Deborah's mind was settled, and she sought to settle Barak's in verses 6 and 7 by sharing God's plan: *"Go and deploy troops at Mount Tabor; take with you ten thousand men of the sons of Naphtali and the sons of Zebulun; and against you I will deploy Sisera, the commander of Jabin's army, with his chariots and multitude at the River Kishon; and I will deliver him into your hand."* Note the words, *"deploy ... and I will deploy"* for they indicate that a sovereign God was in command of His own people and of their enemy. Some other versions translate the Hebrew as, *"draw ... and I will draw,"* Barak took the high ground at Mount Tabor with this assurance in his mind, but Sisera was totally unaware that, though he was leading his forces on the plain of Esdraelon, God was luring him and ready to deliver him. The only similarity in the two men was that neither knew how God would do it. Such is the omnipotence of God that He delivers His own *from* defeat while leading His enemies *to* defeat! Mount Tabor is a notable landmark, and that day, as God unleashed His power, would become part of the reason that *"Tabor and Hermon rejoice in Your name, You have a mighty arm."*[24]

In her song in chapter 5, Deborah recalled the dramatic manner in which

God made Himself known at Sinai in Exodus 19 – *"The earth trembled, the heavens poured, the clouds also poured water. The mountains gushed before the LORD."* Later, in verse 21, she described what happened beneath Mount Tabor, as *"The torrent of Kishon swept them away."* This certainly points to an unseasonal deluge that caught Sisera's troops unprepared for the conditions that overcame them. In the ensuing quagmire, all efforts to retreat proved impossible, the chariots that were seen to be their strength became their weakness, a hindrance rather than a help, and their horses were disabled in the stampede. The army was slain until *"not a man was left,"* yet Sisera had already escaped on foot, as if he alone had evaded the One *"Who makes the clouds His chariot."*[25]

Was Deborah still of *"no other mind"* or did Sisera's escape cause her to doubt? No, she knew from the beginning that it was not God's will for him to be among those whom Barak would capture, and she knew that God would fulfil His word. Faith caused her to live in the expectation, as if he had already said, *"I have purposed it; I will also do it."*[26] And once he had used a woman to complete what He had promised, she could have said, like Jeremiah, *"The LORD has done what He purposed; He has fulfilled His word."*[27]

Most blessed among women

The woman God used was Jael, the wife of Heber, and it is apparent that she didn't share his support of Sisera. L.H. Wiseman says, "It was the company of the faithless Kenites who communicated to the Canaanite commander information of the movements of Barak and his men, and showed Sisera that Barak the son of Abinoam was gone up to mount Tabor. Little may Heber have imagined, while betraying the ancient allies of his fathers, that this treason would be the means of entrapping their mighty enemy to his destruction." Heber was in league with the informers, yet his wife preferred to be numbered with the people of God and lured him into her tent, and to his death. Armed only with a tent peg and hammer she smote the enemy by driving it into his temple, as if to signify that all the plotting of Jabin's hostile mind had come to nothing. Having already gone out to meet the fleeing Sisera, she then went out to meet the pursuing Barak, and there on her tent's floor he saw the evidence: as God had promised, the enemy slain by the hand of a woman.

He had answered, just as He would through Isaiah and Paul, *"I will destroy the wisdom of the wise,"*[28] and though we may wonder at the means, we gladly answer "Yes" to the question, *"Has not God made foolish the wisdom of this world?"* We bow to acknowledge that, through a man who initially was weak in faith and through a woman as the weaker vessel,[29] He *"has chosen the weak things of the world to put to shame the things which are mighty."*[30] As they recognised this for themselves, Deborah and Barak sang chapter 5 in unison, *"I, even I, will sing to the LORD; I will sing praise to the LORD God of Israel."* They were as one voice, with not the slightest trace of superiority or inferiority.

Listen to her as she exalts him: *"Awake, awake, Deborah! Awake, awake, sing a song! Arise, Barak, and lead your captives away, O son of Abinoam!"* Listen again, as they sing about Jael: *"Most blessed among women is Jael, the wife of Heber ... Blessed is she among women in tents."* There was no jealousy in either of them for the simple reason that they had fulfilled their part for the Lord, and she fulfilled hers. Her tent floor was an extension to their battlefield, and they had mutual admiration for a woman who struck the final blow in the same battle.

Chapter 5 Questions

1. Deborah is a good example of a woman whose life was influenced and shaped by former leaders like Othniel and Ehud. How does the New Testament help to shape your life, as you *"Remember those who led you, who spoke the word of God to you"* (Heb.13:7 NASB)?
2. Which aspects of spiritual motherliness have benefitted you, and what others would you like to see in your church (see Tit.2:3-5)?
3. How does fulfilling a God-honouring role emphasise your freedom in Christ and show there is no chauvinistic intent in Christian service?
4. In what ways have you been able to share in helping young men in their spiritual character and growth, as in Titus 2:6-8, and to be supportive of older men, as in 1 Timothy 5:1?
5. Feminism has a strong voice in today's world, so how do you as a Christian woman keep to being of *"no other mind"* (Gal.5:10) in your sense of freedom and fulfilment through the gospel?
6. Describe ways in which God is making you *"blessed among women"* (Judg.5:24) and using you for the blessing of others.

Chapter 6: Abigail

"Now there was a man in Maon whose business was in Carmel, and the man was very rich. He had three thousand sheep and a thousand goats. And he was shearing his sheep in Carmel. The name of the man was Nabal, and the name of his wife Abigail. And she was a woman of good understanding and beautiful appearance; but the man was harsh and evil in his doings. And he was of the house of Caleb" (1 Sam.25:2,3).

Two verses could hardly be more different. The first, in 1 Samuel 25:2, tells us about a man and what he did. The second, in 1 Samuel 25:3, describes a woman and what she was. Being a married couple they should have been enjoying the closest possible earthly bond, but their characters marked them out as being poles apart. Evidently, it was a marriage that had lost any attraction it ever possessed, and now even the meaning of their names showed the gulf between them. For some unknown reason, his parents had called him Nabal, which means a fool or stupid; whereas, hers chose the more hopeful, Abigail, the father or the source of joy.

Married they may have been, but there was no blending of their natures: he was a fool and churlish to the end, while in the purpose of God she became the source of David's joy. And there was only one reason for it: she was a woman God moved, and he was a man who wasn't! He was a man with plenty of goods, but no goodness; with abundance of wealth, but no wisdom. His richest possession was his wife, and he didn't know it. Solomon would write later, *"Houses and riches are an inheritance from fathers, but a prudent wife is from the LORD."*[1] Nabal was so wrapped up in his wealth that he lost interest in his wife, and, under the judgment of God, he lost both.

As we take in the stark connection between verses 2 and 3, it is worth noting that both flow out of verse 1 – *"Then Samuel died; and the Israelites gathered together and lamented for him, and buried him at his home in Ramah. And David arose and went down to the Wilderness of Paran."* We could almost say that his timing was as critical as his arrival in the Vale of Elah where he would not hold back from slaying Goliath. His arrival in Maon and Carmel also carried great significance for it caused him to hold back from slaying Nabal. At Elah, God provided him to do the right thing when a man, King Saul, failed to stand up and be counted. At Carmel, God prevented him from doing the wrong thing when a woman was willing to stand up and be counted. She was wonderfully moved by God to keep David from a huge mistake that would have stained his character and marred his reputation. In a most remarkable way, she gave David the kind of counsel that Samuel would have given him, and unwittingly proved that His hand was on her for David's good. His arrival in the region of Nabal's inheritance followed the loss of his great friend and prophetic counsellor, but he was about to discover that God had shaped a woman to give him good advice. She had no prophetic calling like Samuel, but had a vital ministry to fulfil, nevertheless.

Maon and Carmel are associated with Caleb and the tribe of Judah in Joshua 15:13,54-55, and 1 Samuel 25:3 says Nabal *"was of the house of*

Caleb." There's no doubt that he came from a good background, but, just as the New Testament tells us, *"They are not all Israel who are of Israel,"*[2] we can safely assume that they are not all like Caleb who are of Caleb. Nabal definitely wasn't! God thought highly of Caleb: *"My servant Caleb, because he has a different spirit in him and has followed Me fully, I will bring into the land where he went, and his descendants shall inherit it."*[3] Sadly, He couldn't say that about Nabal, and his hard-heartedness made life unpleasant for his wife. Matthew Henry summed up their situation by saying, "Wisdom is good with an inheritance, but an inheritance is good for little without wisdom. Many an Abigail is tied to a Nabal." How true!

Life can become so much more difficult, sometimes unbearable, for a godly wife who discovers she is more spiritually committed than her husband, and that her appetite for God finds no kindred spirit in him. Some dear sisters have entered into marriage with high hopes and good intentions based on great promises, only to discover the painful truth that these promises were never kept, and their hopes and intentions cruelly dashed. May God help them, like Abigail, to be moved by Him, because He sees something present in them that is absent in their husbands.

In contrast to Nabal, everything Abigail said and did flowed out of what God said about her in verse 3: *"And she was a woman of [1] good understanding and [2] beautiful [3] appearance, but the man was harsh and evil in his doings."* At first glance, this may describe the lovely combination of what she was inwardly and outwardly, but together they emphasise her overall goodness. The first word, *sekel*, gives us a sense of how intelligent, circumspect, wise, and discreet, she was. The second, *wīphat* from *yāphāh*, implies she was bright, comely and pleasant; and the third, *to'ar*, while describing her appearance, causes us to realise that, like Joseph, she could be called *"a goodly person."*[4] She was good-looking, but we are intended to appreciate that her beauty was much more than skin deep!

There is no doubt whatsoever that Nabal was successful at animal husbandry, but it's equally clear he was a complete failure at being a husband. He was very profitable in the first, totally unprofitable in the second. In fact, he probably spent so much time caring for his sheep that he spent no time caring for his wife. Certainly, there would be no time to spare on anyone or anything while shearing three thousand sheep. While being fully committed to doing each of them a favour by releasing it from the weight and heat of its fleece, Nabal was in no mood to show favour to David's men. Their threefold greeting of *"Peace,"* as if on his person, his possessions and property, fell on deaf ears. Not only so, he harshly dismissed the mention of David's name in such a belittling manner: *"Who is David, and who is the son of Jesse?"* His character probably shaped his attitude, but his antagonism may also indicate that he was one of Saul's sympathisers.

A woman of good understanding

Caught in the middle of such a dilemma, Abigail faced up to the reality that wisdom sometimes has to walk a tightrope and face what seems to be impossible.

> Got any rivers you think are uncrossable?
> Got any mountains you can't tunnel through?
> God specialises in things thought impossible
> He does the things others cannot do.
> God is the same and His Word is dependable,
> He'll make a way through the waters for you;

Life's situations by Him are amendable,
Mountains and hills He will part for you too.
(Oscar C. Eliason)

On the one hand, she had marital loyalty to a man whose life she wanted to save, and did; on the other, she had spiritual loyalty to the man God had moved directly or indirectly to save her life and his. After all, had he not conquered the giant Goliath for their sakes, and for their future, as much as for those who stood in the valley *"dismayed and greatly afraid"*[5] Apart altogether from massive defects in his character, Nabal's attitude to David was spawned in lack of appreciation for what David had done for him and, no doubt, Abigail was well aware of that fact. As a couple, they send out a monumental warning to married Christian women: your husband will have nothing to contribute to your spiritual happiness until he has a love for Christ. And he will never be able to give the right sort of lead in your marriage unless he has been led to, and is being led by, the Man of Calvary.

* The wisdom of her attention

Wisdom takes full account of the truth and makes a right assessment of it before reacting to the situation. When one of Nabal's young men spoke to Abigail she drank in the facts regarding how David's men had approached him – on the basis of the word *bārak*, as if to kneel before him in blessing. Nabal took full advantage of them and 'reviled' them and, according to the young man's choice of word, described him as flying at them and swooping like a bird of prey. He then reported what they had done: *"The men were very good to us ... They were a wall to us both by night and day."* In effect, he was saying that they had been especially pleasant and effectively protective. As she listened, Abigail began objectively to form her response, but then the young man warned her of the consequences that Nabal was about to face. Suddenly, his appeal to her turned into his assessment of him: *"For he is such a scoundrel that one cannot speak to him."* Immediately, without adding to or taking away from what he had said, she subjectively accepted his account and rushed off willingly to prepare the kind of gift for David that her husband had so wilfully withheld.

* The wisdom of her presentation

With her bountiful gift securely *"loaded ... on donkeys,"* her servants went ahead of her not only to intercept David and his four hundred men who were intent on slaying every male belonging to Nabal, but to placate him. Significantly, in verse 19, *"she did not to tell her husband Nabal,"* and made the same decision in verse 36, whereas in verse 37 she *"told him these things,"* and the record is, *"his heart died within him, and he became like a stone."* In her wisdom, she knew when to speak and when not to speak. It was as if she acted on Solomon's words long before he wrote them in Proverbs 26:4 and 5: *"Do not answer a fool according to his folly, lest you also be like him. Answer a fool according to his folly, lest he be wise in his own eyes."* Abigail knew how, when and why to do both.

For the second time, she hurried that she might go toward David and humbly cast herself down at his feet, undoubtedly trusting like Jacob entreating Esau, *"I will appease him with the present that goes before me, and afterward I will see his face; perhaps he will accept me."*[6] How wisely she proved that *"out of the abundance of the heart the mouth speaks"*![7] As she lay prostrate before him, her voice rose to still his troubled mind, as surely as his great grandmother Ruth's had quieted Naomi. Naomi arrived in Bethlehem having silently digested Ruth's commitment, and we may wonder if she chastised herself for what she had said on the journey, and what she hadn't. After all, she could have discouraged

Orpah from going back to ungodliness, and encouraged Ruth to go forward to godliness? Along with other poor decisions she had made in the past, the journey home added to her reasons for saying, *"Call me Mara,"*[8] bitterness instead of sweetness. Abigail's appeal, so different from the Moabitess, but equally heartfelt, touched the heart of her future husband and king, and God moved a man by a woman God moved.

"So she fell at his feet and said: "On me, my lord, on me let this iniquity be! And please let your maidservant speak in your ears, and hear the words of your maidservant. Please, let not my lord regard this scoundrel Nabal. For as his name is, so is he: Nabal is his name, and folly is with him! But I, your maidservant, did not see the young men of my lord whom you sent. Now therefore, my lord, as the LORD lives and as your soul lives, since the LORD has held you back from coming to bloodshed and from avenging yourself with your own hand, now then, let your enemies and those who seek harm for my lord be as Nabal. And now this present which your maidservant has brought to my lord, let it be given to the young men who follow my lord.

"Please forgive the trespass of your maidservant. For the LORD will certainly make for my lord an enduring house, because my lord fights the battles of the LORD, and evil is not found in you throughout your days. Yet a man has risen to pursue you and seek your life, but the life of my lord shall be bound in the bundle of the living with the LORD your God; and the lives of your enemies He shall sling out, as from the pocket of a sling. And it shall come to pass, when the LORD has done for my lord according to all the good that He has spoken concerning you, and has appointed you ruler over Israel, that this will be no grief to you, nor offense of heart to my lord, either that you have shed blood without cause,

or that my lord has avenged himself. But when the LORD has dealt well with my lord, then remember your maidservant."[9]

What a model appeal! It had humility: shown outwardly at his feet, and inwardly six times as his maidservant. It also had dignity in calling him "lord," honesty about her husband's folly, liberty in claiming that it was the Lord who kept him from bloodshed – and not her! It had the liberality of her gift, which she intentionally stated was *"brought to my lord"* that it might be *"given to the young men who follow my lord."* She could simply have said it was for them, but she wanted him to know that her present was, in fact, a blessing – *habb^eraākāh* – with *bārak* at its core to show that she was kneeling before him in her heart. Isn't this a lovely example of how we give to the Lord for the benefit of those who follow Him?

Finally, her appeal had a real sense of identity in two particular ways. It related to him historically when she said that God would deal with his enemies: *"He shall sling* [them] *out, as from the pocket of a sling."* David must have seen the connection with Elah and marvelled at a woman who spoke his kind of language. It also related to him prophetically when she said that God would make for him *"an enduring house."* As an appeal, it had all of these, as she carefully wove it into his past, his present, and his future, yet she mentioned none of them. Instead, she focused on *"iniquity"* in verse 24 and her *"trespass"* in verse 28, neither of which David saw in her, though he was impressed by all the others.

In response, he leaned heavily on the word *bārak* and claimed it in a fourfold embrace in verses 32,33 and 39: *"Blessed is the LORD God of Israel, who sent you this day to meet me! And blessed is your advice and blessed are you, because you have kept me this day from coming to bloodshed and from avenging myself with my own hand. Blessed be the LORD, who has pleaded the cause of my reproach."*

David recognised that events could have turned out very badly, and assured Abigail in verse 34 how different the outcome would have been *"unless you had hurried."* Had she not hurried, she would have missed all this blessing, and she causes us to ask how ready we are to respond to our King and enter into His blessing. Perhaps, right now, you are weighing up how you should respond to something you could do for Him. If so, let David's words help you to see that there is a way into further blessing in the service of God that you could miss – *"unless you had hurried."*

What a delightful picture it all is: servants figuratively on their knees at the beginning; a woman similarly on hers in the middle; and David in the self-same spirit at the end! But it was not the end, not yet. There was one more visit to Abigail. This time, trusted servants came with an unexpected invitation: *"David sent us to you, to ask you to become his wife."* Her response was as immediate and emphatic as before: *"Here is your maidservant, a servant to wash the feet of the servants of my lord."* For the third time, she *"rose in haste ... and she followed the messengers of David, and became his wife."* Definitely, a woman God moved, and worth emulating!

* * *

1 Samuel 25:24-42

v.24 "So she fell at his feet and said, 'On me, on me let this iniquity be! And please let your maidservant speak in your ears, and hear the words

of your maidservant.'"
    PRESENT – HUMILITY
    ABSENT – PRIDE

v.25 "Please, let not my lord regard this scoundrel Nabal. For as his name is, so is he: Nabal is his name, and folly is with him! But I, your maidservant, did not see the young men of my lord whom you sent."
    PRESENT – DIGNITY OF HONESTY, OPENNESS
    ABSENT – DECEPTION OF HERSELF AND OTHERS, HATE

v.26 "Now therefore, my lord, as the LORD lives and as your soul lives, since the LORD has held you back from coming to bloodshed and from avenging yourself with your own hand, now then, let your enemies and those who seek harm for my lord be as Nabal."
    PRESENT –SPIRITUALITY, INSIGHT, PEACEABLE
    ABSENT – CARNALITY, SPITE

v.27 "And now this present which your maidservant has brought to my lord, let it be given to the young men who follow my lord."
    PRESENT – GENEROSITY
    ABSENT – SELFISHNESS

v.28 "Please forgive the trespass of your maidservant. For the LORD will certainly make for my lord an enduring house, because my lord fights the battles of the LORD, and evil is not found in you throughout your days."
    PRESENT – LIBERALITY, SENSITIVITY, DISCERNMENT, IDENTITY (PROPHETICALLY)
    ABSENT – GRUDGING, UNCARING

v.29 "Yet a man has risen to pursue you and seek your life, but the life

of my lord shall be bound in the bundle of the living with the LORD your God; and the lives of your enemies He shall sling out, as from the pocket of a sling."
PRESENT - FAITH, ENCOURAGEMENT
ABSENT - DOUBT

v.30 "And it shall come to pass, when the LORD has done for my lord according to all the good that He has spoken concerning you, and has appointed you ruler over Israel ..."
PRESENT - IDENTITY (HISTORICALLY)

v.31 "...that this will be no grief to you, nor offence of heart to my lord, either that you have shed blood without cause, or that my lord has avenged himself. But when the LORD has dealt well with my lord, then remember your maid-servant."
PRESENT - DISCRETION

v.32 "Then David said to Abigail: 'Blessed is the LORD God of Israel, who sent you this day to meet me!'"
PRESENT - HONOUR
ABSENT - SHAME

v.33 "And blessed is your advice and blessed are you, because you have kept me this day from coming to bloodshed and from avenging myself with my own hand."
PRESENT - WISDOM
PRESENT - FOLLY

v.34 "For indeed, as the LORD God of Israel lives, who has kept me back from hurting you, unless you had hurried and come to meet me, surely by morning light no males would have been left to Nabal!"

PRESENT - DILIGENCE
ABSENCE - IMPATIENCE

v.35 "So David received from her hand what she had brought him, and said to her, 'Go up in peace to your house. See, I have heeded your voice and respected your person.'"
PRESENT - KINDNESS

v.36 "Now Abigail went to Nabal, and there he was, holding a feast in his house, like the feast of a king. And Nabal's heart was merry within him, for he was very drunk; therefore she told him nothing, little or much, until morning light."

v.37 "So it was, in the morning, when the wine had gone from Nabal, and his wife had told him these things, that his heart died within him, and he became like a stone."
PRESENT: CONSIDERATION
ABSENCE: CONFRONTATION

v.38 "Then it happened, after about ten days, that the LORD struck Nabal, and he died."

v.39 "So when David heard that Nabal was dead, he said, 'Blessed be the LORD, who has pleaded the cause of my reproach from the hand of Nabal, and has kept His servant from evil! For the LORD has returned the wickedness of Nabal on his own head.' And David sent and proposed to Abigail, to take her as his wife.'"
PRESENT - COMMUNICATION

v.40 "When the servants of David had come to Abigail at Carmel, they spoke to her saying, 'David sent us to you, to ask you to become his wife.'

PRESENT - SUITABLE

v.41 "Then she arose, bowed her face to the earth, and said, 'Here is your maidservant, a servant to wash the feet of the servants of my lord.'"

PRESENT - RESPECT

v.42 "So Abigail rose in haste and rode on a donkey, attended by five of her maidens; and she followed the messengers of David, and became his wife."

PRESENT - SUBJECTION

Chapter 6 Questions

QUESTIONS FOR SINGLES

Everything Abigail said and did flowed out of what God said about her in verse 3: *"And she was a woman of [1] good understanding and [2] beautiful [3] appearance, but the man was harsh and evil in his doings. He was of the house of Caleb."*

1. Understanding: Hebrew *sekel* – intelligent, discreet, wise, circumspect
2. Beautiful: Hebrew *yāphāh* – bright, comely, pleasant
3. Appearance: Hebrew *to'ar* – figure, form

1. Using what we find out about her from these meanings, and from her godly approach in 1 Samuel 25:24-42, discuss how you interact with others.

   a) Are you honest with them? (v.25)

   b) How do they benefit from your spirituality? (v.26)

   c) Are you an encourager? (v.29)

   d) Are you wise in the way you challenge or confront people? For instance in what you say, how you say it, and when you say it? (vv.36,37)

   e) How do you rate your communication skills? e.g.

* in normal conversation
* in sharing concerns (open or bottled-up?)
* in discussing a problem
* in a disagreement
f) In what ways can others detect your subjection?

2. Nabal's nature must have been a disappointment to Abigail, and he must have been very difficult to live with. What do you think about her openness with David in verse 25? She could have reacted to her marriage problems by letting herself go spiritually, temperamentally and physically, but she didn't. How do you prevent letting yourself go?

3. Being of the house of Caleb means that Nabal came from a good family background. It also means he didn't live up to his reputation or to her expectation. How would you handle it if anyone let you down like this?

QUESTIONS FOR MARRIEDS

Everything Abigail said and did flowed out of what God said about her in verse 3: "*And she was a woman of [1] good understanding and [2] beautiful [3] appearance, but the man was harsh and evil in his doings. He was of the house of Caleb.*"

1. Understanding: Hebrew *sekel* – intelligent, discreet, wise, circumspect
2. Beautiful: Hebrew *yāphāh* – bright, comely, pleasant
3. Appearance: Hebrew *to'ar* – figure, form

1. Using what we find out about her from these meanings, and from her godly approach in 1 Samuel 25:24-42, discuss how you interact with your husband.

a) Are you honest with him? (v.25)

b) How does he benefit from your spirituality? (v.26)

c) Do you know when he's down? Are you an encourager? (v.29)

d) Are you wise in the way you challenge or confront him? e.g. in what you say, how you say it, and when you say it? (vv.36,37)

e) How do you rate your communication skills with each other? e.g.

* in normal conversation

* in sharing concerns (open or bottled-up?)

* in discussing a problem

* in a disagreement

f) In what ways can he detect your subjection to him?

2. Nabal's nature must have been a disappointment to Abigail, and he must have been very difficult to live with. What do you think about her openness with David in verse 25? Did her honesty breach her subjection? She could have reacted to her marriage problems by letting herself go spiritually, temperamentally and physically, but she didn't. How do you prevent letting yourself go?

3. Being of the house of Caleb means that Nabal came from a good family background. It also means that he didn't live up to his reputation or to her expectation. How would you handle this kind of let-down?

Chapter 7: A Certain Woman

"A certain woman of the wives of the sons of the prophets cried out to Elisha, saying, 'Your servant my husband is dead, and you know that your servant feared the LORD. And the creditor is coming to take my two sons to be his slaves.' So Elisha said to her, 'What shall I do for you? Tell me, what do you have in the house?' And she said, 'Your maidservant has nothing in the house but a jar of oil.' Then he said, 'Go, borrow vessels from everywhere, from all your neighbors — empty vessels; do not gather just a few. And when you have come in, you shall shut the door behind you and your sons; then pour it into all those vessels, and set aside the full ones.' So she went from him and shut the door behind her and her sons, who brought the vessels to her; and she poured it out. Now it came to pass, when the vessels were full, that she said to her son, 'Bring me another vessel.' And he said to her, 'There is not another vessel.' So the oil ceased. Then she came and told the man of God. And he said, 'Go, sell the oil and pay your debt; and you and your sons live on the rest'" (2 Kin.4:1-7).

There's something specially endearing when we see God turning from being the Victor in Israel's national battle against the enemy on the battlefield to become the victor in a widow's personal struggle in her home. Such is the contrast between 2 Kings 3 and 4. Jehoshaphat, king of Judah, knew the value of the reassuring voice of God and rested on the promise that came through prophetic ministry: *"Do not be afraid nor dismayed because of this great multitude, for the battle is not yours, but God's."*[1] The conflict in 2 Kings 3 found him asking the all-important question, *"Is there no prophet of the LORD here, that we may inquire of the LORD by him?"* It's not in the least surprising that Jehoram, the faithless king of Israel, had nothing to say, but one of his servants knew the answer: *"Elisha the son of Shaphat is here."* How good it is when an unexpected source knows what the expected source doesn't, and can see what blind unbelief can't see! Evidently, the dear man couldn't look to his king for an example of military courage, for, not only did he question the direction of their mission, he doubted God's motive in letting them go and concluded, *"Alas! For the LORD has called these three kings together to deliver them into the hand of Moab."* Undaunted by Jehoram's failure, Jehoshaphat heard Elisha's command — *"Thus says the LORD: 'Make this valley full of ditches'"* — and, by faith, neither queried God's motives nor His means.

Doubt sees the obstacles;
Faith sees the way.
Doubt sees the darkest night;
Faith sees the day.
Doubt dreads to take a step
Faith soars on high.
Doubt questions, "Who believes?"
Faith answers, "I!"
(William Harvey Jett)

Changes in God's means are intended as a stimulus to faith for they teach us that, though they vary, He is unchanging. David's triumph over

Goliath didn't make him dependent on a sling in the future; Shamgar's victory over the Philistines didn't cause others to use an ox goad in their conflicts; and Samson threw away the jawbone of a donkey that had been so effective against a thousand men, rather than keep it for further conquests. Similarly, God's means for His people's battles varied. In one, they were told, *"You will not need to fight in this battle. Position yourselves, stand still and see the salvation of the LORD, who is with you."*[2] In 2 Kings 3, with no water for the thirsty troops who had dug the trenches, *"The next morning, about the time of offering the sacrifice, behold, water came ... till the country was filled with water."*[3] This was a monumental lesson for them, that God's timing was packed with meaning as He linked their provision on the battlefield with the presentation of the morning lamb on the altar in His temple.[4]

How perfectly His timing and teaching combine to show that the offering of the lamb and the triumph of His people go together! It was such an important lesson He wanted them to learn that, if they were right with Him at the altar, He would be right with them in the arena of their battles. God sowed this vital truth in the Old Testament knowing it would come to full fruition in the New, and Romans 8:3 spells it out so clearly. The triumph of the cross is summed up by this, *"For what the law could not do in that it was weak through the flesh, God did by sending His own Son in the likeness of sinful flesh, on account of sin: He condemned sin in the flesh,"* and the remainder of the letter assures us that the Christian's triumph is wrapped up in it, too. Christ the Victor, ours the victory!

Your servant my husband is dead

Returning from the scene of national need where an answer of peace had depended on a word from the LORD through him, the next appeal Elisha heard came from a heartbroken widow whose personal battle was just as real. It was no ordinary cry for the dear woman's shriek (Heb. *tsā‘ᵃqāh*) carried the distress of her heart to his, and he ministered to her on her doorstep with the same sense of leaning on God who was about to show that personal victory on the home-front was as much assured as national victory on the battlefront.

Scriptural examples are readily found of the people collectively crying to God, sometimes expressed by the word *zā‘aq*, but still with the urgency and fervency of a shriek. It says of some tribes in 1 Chronicles 5:20, *"And they were helped ... for they cried out to God in the battle. He heeded their prayer, because they put their trust in Him."* Individuals also had a similar experience, as Asaph describes in Psalm 77:2 – *"I cried [from tsā‘aq] out to God with my voice—To God with my voice; and He gave ear to me. In the day of my trouble I sought the LORD; my hand was stretched out in the night without ceasing; my soul refused to be comforted."*

The sense of grappling with an unbearable burden was so real to the psalmist, and no less so to the woman, but she hadn't altogether lost her composure. Note how she called out to Elisha: *"Your servant my husband is dead, and you know that your servant feared the LORD."* His relationship with God through His servant came first, then his relationship with her. The spiritual bond preceded the natural. She could have said, "My husband your servant is dead," and we would have thought no less of her. Alternatively, she might have put it this way: "I am the wife of your servant who has died, and I know that my husband feared the LORD." Undoubtedly, this would have been true, but she chose to emphasise

71

that the prophet who knew the mind of the LORD also knew the mindset of his servant, and it was better to rest on his estimation of him than her own. Her married life had been blessed through a genuinely godly man whose reverence for God was known, not only among the sons of the prophets, but by her in their home-life. It is essential that the woman who knows him best unreservedly shares a husband's standing among his brethren! Anything different, makes marriage much more difficult; and, sadly, it has become an unbearable burden for some.

Luke tells us that the Lord was well-attended by *"certain women,"* meaning they were all of a kind. In their case, He had healed them from demon-possession and other disabilities, and they responded by following Him and ministering to Him and His disciples. In 2 Kings 4, the word *"certain"* indicates one woman, but it comes from *'echād* which can mean one in the sense of being united. It was first used to describe Adam and Eve's oneness in marriage in Genesis 2:24, and there is no doubt that the woman who cried out to Elisha had enjoyed being united in the marriage bond with her God-centred husband. Now it was over, and she was doing her utmost to keep herself and her family together: bereaved, bankrupt, but believing. At a time when everything seemed to be falling apart, she truly was a united woman whose faith was not unravelling. The man to whom she was so indebted had left her in debt and, with the dreaded sound of the lender's knock shortly to be heard on her door, she manifestly believed that the grace of God through the man of God could overcome the obligation she faced under the law of God. With no means of paying, her only collateral was her two sons whose future was in danger of being commandeered as servants until the next Year of Jubilee.[5] It was grief added to grief and, being utterly helpless under the demands of the law, grace was her only means of release and ever being able to say, *"He has redeemed my soul in peace from the battle that was against me."*[6]

The way she thought

This woman's character and reputation must have been well known to Elisha for his offer of help was immediate and favourable, as seen in his questions, *"What shall I do for you? Tell me, what do you have in the house?"* He certainly thought more of her than he did of the king of Israel. When he came for help with Jehoshaphat and the king of Edom, Elisha had a very different question and dismissive statement for him: *"What have I to do with you? Go to the prophets of your father and the prophets of your mother."* Jehoram had the audacity to repeat his faithless assertion that Jehovah had *"called these three kings together to deliver them into the hand of Moab."* Had this been true, the prophet would have had no option but to confirm the mind of the Lord. However, troubled by such a Godless claim, he let him know exactly where he stood before him and before God: *"As the LORD of hosts lives, before whom I stand, surely were it not that I regard the presence of Jehoshaphat king of Judah, I would not look at you, nor see you."* It wasn't that Elisha had become ungracious. No, just as the Lord Jesus Christ did, at times, he spoke in the honesty and frankness of grace.

Had Israel's king come in the lowly spirit of the widow, he would have heard words of reassuring grace as she did. She began by seeing her husband as a servant, she continued by not wanting to see her sons become servants, and she finished by referring to herself as a servant. Elisha had good reason to 'look' at her and 'see' her. She and her husband had mirrored each other's servant character in oneness that would have allowed them to say, *"Unite my heart to fear Your name."*[7] They were two of a kind: at one in affection and dedication. Can you say this about your husband and yourself, and hold on to the desire that your family will never be servants of anyone but the Lord?

The way she felt

Poverty is a great test of faith, and Elisha's question – *"Tell me, what do you have in the house?"* – must have made her wonder how any means of help could come from what she had available. She could have so easily answered, "Nothing, but a jar of oil," but she didn't. Remaining humble and dependent, she replied, *"Your maidservant has nothing in the house but a jar of oil."* Would God work a second time for a poor widow, as He had done years earlier through Elijah? How faithfully He responds when His children have nothing, and we can be encouraged humbly to depend upon Him, too!

The Lord Jesus proved this when twice He fed two different multitudes who had *"nothing to eat,"*[8] and twice came to the aid of His disciples when they went fishing and *"caught nothing."*[9] Later, the same faithful God testified to the church in Corinth when Paul spoke about being *"sorrowful, yet always rejoicing; as poor, yet making many rich; as having nothing, and yet possessing all things."*[10] The contrast could hardly be greater: nothing to hold on to, materially; holding on to everything, spiritually. It was for this reason that the Lord Jesus Christ could say to the church in Smyrna, *"I know your ... poverty (but you are rich),"*[11] and Paul could say of the churches of Macedonia, *"that in a great trial of affliction the abundance of their joy and their deep poverty abounded in the riches of their liberality."*[12] In similar grace, God was about to show that *"He relieves the fatherless and widow"*[13] by turning her trial from sorrow to joy, and from deep poverty to the riches of liberality.

The way she listened

Unlike Peter who replied, *"Not so, Lord!"* when God told him to *"Rise … kill and eat,"*[14] this woman was commanded, *"Go, borrow … shut … and pour … So she went … and shut … brought … and she poured."* There was no hesitation. There were no questions. Grace had spoken, and faith obeyed. Having done this in the privacy of her own room, not publicly to impress others, she returned to the man of God who followed up his initial fourfold command with another: *"Go, sell … pay your debt, and … live,"* and miraculously her debt was gone. In the strangeness of God's ways, as strange as digging trenches in a valley had been in chapter 3, borrowing had been the cause and borrowing had become the cure. Poverty had turned from being her master to being her servant, and being in debt led to being indebted. Her disappointment had become His appointment; her disadvantage became His advantage; and her discontentment was turned to His contentment.

A mother's example

With the creditor's threat gone she must have rejoiced in being a very united woman! Having been united in godliness with her husband in marriage and family life, with her boys in the grief of bereavement, and with them in debt, they now shared in being united with her in the joy of deliverance. Faith replaced fear, and living in ensured unison replaced leaving and enforced separation. She had taught them by early example what God would say through Jeremiah, *"Leave your fatherless children, I will preserve them alive; and let your widows trust in Me."*[15] By unforgettable means, they learned that, *"A father of the fatherless, a defender of widows, is God in His holy habitation."*[16] They had known the reality of access to God inside their own closed door: they were shut off from outside, shut in with Him, and the creditor's threat was shut out.

Had she been like Lot in Genesis 19:4-11, when evil men surrounded his house to harm his visitors, she would have shut the door from the outside that she might stand there to negotiate with those she feared. Not only that, she would have needed other hands to reach out to pull her inside so that they could shut the door for her. In the wisdom and comfort of her level of personal godliness and spiritual dependence, she knew that she needed faith's transaction with God and not fear's conciliation with the foe. Being settled with her Comforter was a much greater priority than having a settlement with the creditor. On a similar occasion, in 2 Kings 6:30-33, when a king sent his messenger to take Elisha's life and, being forewarned by God, told the elders who were with him, *"Do you see how this son of a murderer has sent someone to take away my head? Look, when the messenger comes, shut the door, and hold him fast at the door. Is not the sound of his master's feet behind him?"* In a very real way, Elisha was re-enacting what the woman had discovered from his advice: the door must be shut on adversity, if the door of faith is to be opened for our security.

Each of us has a very personal decision to make regarding how prayerfully we deal with the various spiritual battles that confront us. Either we shut the door to be shut in with God and to keep the adversary out or we fail to shut the door and let him in. The Lord Jesus Christ spoke of our great need for privacy with God, as part of His 'Sermon on the Mount' in Matthew 6:6 — *"But you, when you pray, go into your room, and when you have shut your door, pray to your Father who is in the secret place; and your Father who sees in secret will reward you openly."* He couldn't have been more personal and direct for, speaking always in the singular, He focused on your prayer, your room, your door, your Father, and your reward. Three times over, in verses 4, 6 and 18, He also tells us that our Father *"sees in secret."* But what does He see? Firstly, He sees you; secondly, He sees your prayer-burden; thirdly, He sees into your room;

and, fourthly, He sees your shut door. Now we may ask how often does He see? Our answer has to be as personal as His promise, and entirely depends on the answer to another question that each of us must ask. How often is my 'when'?

Emerging from her re-opened door with provision for her neighbours whose vessels had been filled, her faith progressed still farther until she had full payment of her debt and plenty oil remaining for her own family. God had answered in as unexpected a manner as He had for Jehoram and Jehoshaphat's armies. No trenches were dug in her home, yet its floors were packed with empty vessels waiting to be filled by another divine outpouring. Gathering pots and pans, basins and bowls from neighbours was a human work, but the oil they took back was the evidence of a work of God. Perhaps this holds a gospel lesson for us all, that we may draw different benefits from those who live near us, but what blessing do we take to them that introduces them to *"the Holy Spirit, whom* [God] *poured out on us abundantly through Jesus Christ our Saviour"?*[17] As far as the woman is concerned, she became the witness of a rewarding God to her boys, of blessing to her neighbours, and to a creditor who expected to reap the benefit of her bondage rather than full payment of debt through her freedom.

> God moves in a mysterious way
> His wonders to perform
> He plants His footsteps in the sea
> And rides upon the storm.
>
> Ye fearful saints, fresh courage take
> The clouds you so much dread
> Are big with mercy and shall break
> In blessings on your head.
> (William Cowper)

Chapter 7 Questions

1. How do you take the intended spiritual comfort from 1 Chronicles 20:15 – *"Do not be afraid nor dismayed ... for the battle is not yours, but God's"* – while being really aware that you are facing a real struggle?

2. Answered prayer means so much to believers, but how do you make sure that it leads to a deeper appreciation of the Lamb and His work on the cross?

3. What lessons do you draw from this woman that help you to become a more united woman?

4. Servanthood meant a lot to her, both in regard to her husband and herself. In what sort of ways would their reverence for God strengthen their marriage, and what help should this have been to their boys?

5. Elisha was good at taking his own advice, as we saw in 2 Kings 4:4, 33 and 6:32. How can we apply it to the all-important matter of having a private place where we *"shut the door"* and having access to the *"secret place"*?

Chapter 8: A Notable Woman

"Now it happened one day that Elisha went to Shunem, where there was a notable woman, and she persuaded him to eat some food. So it was, as often as he passed by, he would turn in there to eat some food. And she said to her husband, 'Look now, I know that this is a holy man of God, who passes by us regularly. Please, let us make a small upper room on the wall; and let us put a bed for him there, and a table and a chair and a lampstand; so it will be, whenever he comes to us, he can turn in there.' And it happened one day that he came there, and he turned in to the upper room and lay down there.

"Then he said to Gehazi his servant, 'Call this Shunammite woman.' When he had called her, she stood before him. And he said to him, 'Say now to her, "Look, you have been concerned for us with all this care. What can I do for you? Do you want me to speak on your behalf to the king or to the commander of the army?"' She answered, 'I dwell among my own people.' So he said, 'What then is to be done for her?' And Gehazi answered, 'Actually, she has no son, and her husband is old.' So he said, 'Call her.' When he had called her, she stood in the doorway. Then he said, 'About this time next year you shall embrace a son.' And she

said, 'No, my lord. Man of God, do not lie to your maidservant!'
But the woman conceived, and bore a son when the appointed
time had come, of which Elisha had told her. And the child grew"
(2 Kin.4:8-18).

A cclaim is never the right reason for serving the Lord, neither is anonymity, but it is better to be commended and not named, than to be named and not commended. In contrast to the poor unnamed woman we thought about in the previous chapter, this woman, also not named, still had her husband, and was rich. It's also likely that she was never able to say to Elisha, "Your servant, my husband is alive," yet there was something very special about her. The word *'great'* that describes her in some Bible versions comes from the word *gādōl*, which also conveys thoughts of being dignified, well-to-do, prominent and notable. So she stood out, but not because she wanted fame or to be in the spotlight.

This is a great lesson in itself for many have fallen at the hurdle of self-promotion and learned the hard way that *"God resists the proud, but gives grace to the humble."*[1] When he was eighteen years old, C. H. Spurgeon was keen to study at Regent's Park College, and an appointment was arranged for him to attend an interview. In spite of rising early so as to be there on time, something went wrong and, missing the interview, he failed to be accepted. This came as a real blow to him, so he went for a walk to mull over his disappointment, and it was then that Jeremiah 45:5 (KJV) came to him – *"Seekest thou great things for thyself? Seek them not!"* The word spoke to him and, in spite of the setback, he became known as 'The Prince of Preachers.'

As far as this woman was concerned, her aspirations went no higher than to serve, and her humility is the first notable feature that draws our attention. Although it was her open door that admitted Elisha, it was her opened eyes and heart that recognised him as a holy man of God. Lesser eyes could have focused on his physical appearance, but God in His goodness had shaped her life by blessing the eyes of her heart with godly perception. She was so affected by seeing him going past the outside of her house that she wanted to have him stay on the inside. There is no doubt that God moved her for this very reason, and her story goes on to show that her godly responses flowed from the humility and spirituality of her being.

As we think of things that impressed her, perhaps we should search our hearts by asking if He would move us for the same reason, or if we are attracted by lesser things. It's perfectly natural for friendships to be influenced by commendable human traits, but spiritually minded fellowship grows on the godly features of the new nature, which every Christian should find appealing. Do we, for instance, feel the impact of things that mattered to her?

Impressed by his holiness – v.9

Just by observing, her godly vision led to a godly evaluation of him, and being impressed by his holiness was enough for her to weigh up how she could provide hospitality. By doing this, she became a lovely example of what the New Testament gift of hospitality really is for she used it as a spiritual, yet practical, ministry to a servant of God. Spiritual intent is the vital motivation of all spiritual gifts, so that they are effective in *"building up the body of Christ,"*[2] which means that 'hospitality' is not simply an upgraded natural ability, since the same, or better, could be shown by those who are not *"fellow-heirs, and fellow-members of the body."*[3]

In her case, hospitality went far beyond catering for him when *"he would turn in there to eat some food,"* and so she proposed that she and her husband should make a furnished room on their roof for their regular visitor. By doing this, they became listed among the hosts of Scripture who were blessed with special guests. In 2 Samuel 6:11, *"The ark of the LORD remained in the house of Obed-Edom the Gittite three months. And the LORD blessed Obed-Edom and all his household."* As the symbol of Christ in glory, it was normally kept in the Most Holy Place in the tabernacle, so it was a great honour to have it in his home. But the couple on their way home from Jerusalem to Emmaus in Luke 24:28,29 were more greatly honoured when the Stranger who accompanied them came *"to the village where they were going, and He indicated that He would have gone farther. But they constrained Him, saying, "Abide with us, for it is toward evening, and the day is far spent." And He went in to stay with them."*

The woman in Shunem was very much like Lydia in Acts 16:15 and 40, when she begged Paul and Silas, *"If you have judged me to be faithful to the Lord, come to my house and stay." So she persuaded us ... So they went out of the prison and entered the house of Lydia."* As for the Shunammite's husband, it seems he was compliant enough to do as she suggested, but not spiritual enough to enter into the upcoming blessings of the man of God or the burdens of his wife. It was while he was enjoying the comfort of their room that Elisha wondered how she could be compensated, and offered to arrange some recognition from the king or the commander of the host. By assuring him that she felt settled among her own people, she showed that *"godliness with contentment is great gain,"*[4] and proved that true humility rests itself in the will of God her King and needed no favour from a commander of the host, *sar hatsaābā'*, when it relies on Jehovah of Hosts, *Yahweh ts^e bā'ōt.*

Gehazi wasn't always the most dependable servant, as we find in 2 Kings 5:20-27 when greed caused him to lie in Elisha's name, and then be condemned as a leper by the master he disgraced. However, even the worst of servants can do something right, and he was quick to point out that she had no son when Elisha asked, *"What then is to be done for her?"*

* Impressed by his godliness - v.27

Following his promised birth, the little lad grew and, like any farmer's boy, was keen to be in the field with the workers. When he suddenly became unwell, his father told a servant to *"carry him to his mother,"* and, shortly afterward, he died on her lap. In the first step – the response of faith – she went upstairs, laid him on Elisha's bed, rather than her own, and shut the door, as if leaving her crisis in the hands of God as the source of her apparently miraculous gift. Sadly, there was interest of the wrong kind when she went to the field to ask her husband for a helper and a donkey to take her to the man of God. No question was asked about the boy's condition, and all that concerned him was why she had to go that day. Her simple reply was, *"Shalōm,"* – *"It is well,"* and faith continued its journey toward Mount Carmel.

It's the answer she also gave to Gehazi when he ran to meet her and asked, *"Is it well with you? Is it well with your husband? Is it well with the child?"* How could it be? She was a grieving mother. Her husband had shown no great interest. The boy was lying dead on the man of God's bed, yet faith still said, *"Shalom."* It was only when she reached Elisha that she fell down before him that faith might express itself at his feet. Unable to read her distress, Gehazi tried to push her away, and it was as if the beginning and end of her journey was marked by hindrances to faith. Even when Elisha urged Gehazi to take his staff and lay it *"on the face of the child,"* the Shunammite was instinctively uneasy and refused to leave the prophet's side. Who could blame her? In the reliance of faith, she is such an example to the Christian who cries:

> Jesus, my sorrow lies too deep
> For human ministry;
> It knows not how to tell itself
> To any but to Thee.
> And is it not, O Lord, enough,
> This holy sympathy?
> There is no sorrow e'er so deep
> But I may bring to Thee.
> (Horatius Bonar)

Evidently, if his father had come home and not found him on his bed, he had never thought to look for his son on the man of God's bed. The difference between the mind of faith and the faithless mind is striking for what comes first to the one comes last, if at all, to the other. How sterile were Gehazi's attempts to bring life to the cold form that still lay before him! There he was with the rod of the man of God, had gone at the bidding of the man of God, and followed the instructions of the man of God, and nothing changed. Why? For one reason: he wasn't a man of God!

* Impressed by his power – v.36

Unlike Gehazi, when Elisha arrived he went straight up to his room, shut the door behind him, and prayed. First of all it says, *"He went in,"* and having prayed, *"He went up."* This is where Gehazi critically failed: he never went down before God to pray that the Life-giver would restore life. Elisha also *"stretched himself"* on him. How does a full-grown man do that for a child? Should it not have said that he shrank himself? It was done in utmost humility: mouth to mouth, eyes to eyes, and hands to hands, so that the one through whom life would flow might be completely given to him. It is such a Christlike picture to foreshadow One who was much more than a man of God. He is the God-Man who *"humbled himself and became obedient unto death, even death on a cross."*[5] For your sake and mine, He both humbled Himself and stretched Himself that He might overcome our death through His own death, and give us life through His own life. He is our Elisha – God is salvation.

Having shown the response of faith, and the reliance of faith, the time had come when nothing less than a work of God provided the recompense of faith. The shut door was opened, prayer asked in faith had been answered, a dead boy had come to life, and the woman who *"laid him on the bed of the man of God"* was told to pick up her son. But notice the deference of faith: before doing that, *"She went in, fell at his feet, and bowed to the ground; **then** she picked up her son and went out."* How easily she could have lit up in an attitude of "I got what I wanted," but the gift of faith recognised the Giver before the gifted picked up her gift! She had started at his feet in her grief in verse 27, and she ended there in her gladness in verse 37. In the goodness of God, Elisha had taken her into the realm of what the law could not do. It could pass the sentence of death for sin, but was incapable of giving life, and she knew that grace had intervened. From our present viewpoint, we see it as the gospel in a nutshell.

As the representative of the law and the prophets, Elisha served the One who told His people, *"Turn from your evil ways, and keep My commandments and My statutes, according to all the law which I commanded your fathers, and which I sent to you by My servants the prophets."*[6] Gehazi had gone in the authority of the law, but was unable to work according to the ability of grace. Elisha transcended the limitations of the law to trust in the unlimited grace of the Law-giver, and he reminds us of Paul's question: *"Therefore He who supplies the Spirit to you and works miracles among you, does He do it by the works of the law, or by the hearing of faith?"*[7] How shall we answer such a searching question? God is both the Supplier and the Worker; everything is of Him, and experienced through faith. His is the grace, and His is the power. The Shunammite woman had a foretaste of this, and was suitably impressed by the working of His power. She knew from the start that a holy man of God drew his holiness entirely from God, and in the end she knew that God was the only source of his power. Oh that, as Christians, we might be more impressed by the holiness of God before ever seeking to be impressed by His power! His attributes are indivisible, and only by knowing the power of His holiness can we truly know the holiness of His power.

Sadly, she made faith's journey on her own. The words of Hebrews 3:19–4:2 (NASB), that describe those who failed to enter into God's rest through unbelief, could so readily be applied to her husband: *"the word they heard ... was not united by faith in those who heard."* He was the real tragedy of the day, not the death of their son, for he completely missed out from entering into the rest she had in her faith on the way out, and in the rest she had in God's grace on the way back. He had missed the sense of her burden and, as the result, missed the sense of her blessing, and of being included in Hebrews 11 where verse 35 so pointedly says, *"Women received their dead raised to life again."* The closing verse of her story begins by saying, *"So she went in,"* and ends, *"and went out,"* and the words, *"Go, call your husband, and come here,"*[8] were never uttered! Even so, he had every opportunity to have a personal dealing with God. There's no doubt that God was speaking, yet there is no evidence that he was listening or that he was affected by his wife's notable faith. Had he been more sensitive, he also could have been impressed on at least four occasions.

* The way she saw Elisha – v.9

The old saying can be applied in different ways – "Two men looked out from prison bars, one saw mud, the other stars." It probably was true of this woman and her husband, not only when Elisha was a passer-by, but also after he had frequented their home. Her opinion of him was her own, but this didn't keep her from inferring that her husband's point of view should be included, since he *"passes by us regularly."* Scripture is silent regarding his opinion, though his absence from the main part of her story speaks for itself.

* The way she acted – vv.8,10

She then moved on from voicing what should have been their joint perception to outline what she felt should be their joint intention and joint venture. Once again, Scripture is silent regarding his assent, yet we assume he willingly shared in the practicality of her suggestion, if not in the spirituality of her estimation. She certainly gave him his place by speaking, not only submissively, but inclusively: *"Please"* ... *"let us"* ... *"let us"* ... *"whenever he comes to us."* We have no idea how comfortable or uncomfortable this made him feel, but helpfulness with hammer and nails for the man of God's room may not have stretched to being comfortable about spiritual discussions and prayer in their home. When it came to the latter, the Shunammite probably felt isolated in her marriage, and she may have been able to say, like Solomon, *"There is one alone, without companion."* In her longing for a spiritual counterpart, she could have added, *"Two are better than one,"* and, if this had been true, then with Elisha included, she could have added, *"And a threefold cord is not quickly broken."*[9]

* The way she coped – vv.20,27

Twice over, the notable strength of her character came out in her approach to Elisha, as the Spirit of God drew on the word *chāzaq* to describe her. The first time was at her own doorway when she *"persuaded"* him to come in, and the second was at his place in Mount Carmel when she *"caught him by the feet."* The strength of how she appealed to him was reflected in the strength of how she gripped him, and the prophet would sense that she was never weak or half-hearted. Immediately he knew that her answer, *"It is well,"* to her husband and Gehazi, concealed the anguish that gripped and grieved her soul, since neither of them could relate to her feelings or her faith. Just as she had transmitted the strength of her desire to him at her home, she now transferred the strength of her distress as she grasped his feet.

* The way she thanked him – v.37

There is much to take in as we think of her setting out for the return journey on the same day with the discomfort of another twenty-five miles' trip in the heat, and the comfort of God's peace in her heart. Nor can we enter into the upheaval that went on during the lonely time of waiting, yet we marvel at her demeanour as she entered the room to find her son alive beside the man of God. At the end of his Christlike ministry toward her, he had the servant's joy that the Lord had when He raised a young lad to life and *"gave him back to his mother."*[10] She had shown outstanding compassion when he sat, dying, on her lap; and now she showed outstanding composure as he stood before her alive. Rather than showing ecstatic joy at the sight of him, she first fell on the floor at the feet of the man of God and bowed in worship before her God.

What a witness she was to her boy, and what a remarkable testimony the young servant had to share when he returned to the field!

Sisters, if you are alone in the spiritual side of married life, and presently you feel as if you are caught up in a losing battle, God knows your struggle. He knows if the pleasure of getting married has been replaced by the pain of married life. As one young sister put it, "I am feeling so sad about all these things and am not getting why all this is happening in my life. I just believe in my Heavenly Father who cares for me and shapes my life, which glorifies Him, and I trust our prayers will not go in vain. Moreover, my good Shepherd will lead me in green pastures and even He is praying for me always sitting at the right hand of God. My times are in His hands and He has full control over this." Yes, He knows your feelings, and He also knows your faith. All through His Word, there are men and women who have been moved by Him, and He wants to move you, too. Some of their names are never mentioned, only their character; but how much better it is not to be named and be seen by Him as *"notable,"* than to be named and not be notable!

Chapter 8 Questions

1. This woman is a lovely example of surviving difficult circumstances and surmounting them by faith. Drawing on her experience, how can we increase our faith in its capacity to handle lifelong disappointment, such as in a marriage that has no real spiritual togetherness?
2. As a meaningful part of increasing our faith, how do we deepen its character, as she did, in diligence, dependence, and deference?
3. In what sort of ways does your own 'spiritually minded fellowship' grow as the result of godly features you see in other believers?
4. What is there about the Shunammite's attitude and actions that attracts you to her, and how do you think you can imitate her godly nature?
5. The closing scene depicts her in a lowly spirit of worship. How does your own daily experience of God cause you to enjoy times of worship before Him?

Chapter 9: Choice Women

"The sons of Asher were Imnah, Ishvah, Ishvi, Beriah, and their sister Serah. The sons of Beriah were Heber and Malchiel, who was the father of Birzaith. And Heber begot Japhlet, Shomer, Hotham, and their sister Shua. The sons of Japhlet were Pasach, Bimhal, and Ashvath. These were the children of Japhlet. The sons of Shemer were Ahi, Rohgah, Jehubbah, and Aram. And the sons of his brother Helem were Zophah, Imna, Shelesh, and Amal. The sons of Zophah were Suah, Harnepher, Shual, Beri, Imrah, Bezer, Hod, Shamma, Shilshah, Jithran, and Beera. The sons of Jether were Jephunneh, Pispah, and Ara. The sons of Ulla were Arah, Haniel, and Rizia. All these were the children of Asher, heads of their fathers' houses, choice men, mighty men of valor, chief leaders. And they were recorded by genealogies among the army fit for battle; their number was twenty-six thousand" (1 Chron.7:30-40).

Profiting from the Word can be difficult, but should never be impossible. This is never more true than when we are faced with a seemingly endless list of names, as in the first twelve chapters of 1 Chronicles. Is it worth ploughing through or should we just give up attempting to glean from them? The first thing we notice, simply by reading, is that names matter to God. If we ever doubted this, at least six other genealogies will verify it in Genesis 5, 10 and 11, Ruth 4, Ezra 2, Matthew 1, and Luke 3.

Names

Take 1 Chronicles 1:1, for example: *"Adam, Seth, Enosh."* Immediately, we realise that Cain and Abel were excluded, since neither of them contributed to the line that led to Noah whose family began the re-peopling of the world after the flood. Having lost his perfection through sin in Eden, Adam then lost his first son at the murderous hand of the second outside the garden. After this, Seth, whose name implies a substitute, was born; and Enosh, his firstborn, continued the Adamic line in the character of his name as frail, mortal man. God had begun His rescue mission and, just as only one of Adam's sons led to Noah, so only one of Noah's sons, Shem, would lead on to Abraham. In keeping with the omission of Abel in verse 1, the lines of Japheth and Ham were excluded from those who led to Abraham, Ishmael was not included in the blessing through Isaac nor Esau in the furtherance of God's purpose through Jacob that led onward to the provision of a people for God, a kingdom, and a priesthood. Well might we glean among the names of those whom He has listed in the fulfilment of His purpose!

Actions

Among the names we find comments attached to some that yield thoughts that are worthy of deeper consideration, especially if we apply the threefold route of explore, expand, explain. For example:

- 1:12 - *"Casluhim (from whom came the Philistines)*
- 2:7 - *"Achar, the troubler of Israel"*

- 4:9,10 - The prayer of Jabez
- 4:14 - *Joab the father of Ge Harashim, for they were craftsmen.*
- 4:21 - *... and the families of the house of the linen workers*
- 4:23 - *These were the potters ... there they dwelt with the king for his work.*
- 5:20 - *... for they cried out to God in the battle. He heeded their prayer, because they put their trust in Him.*

These brief words of irrefutable testimony cement thoughts of divine approval or disapproval and give a valuable lead into further study of God's detailed assessment and record of individual names and actions. They also prove that *"The eyes of the LORD are in every place, keeping watch on the evil and the good,"*[1] and serve to remind us that our names and actions are always before Him. The day is coming when *"We must all appear before the judgment seat of Christ, that each one may receive the things done in the body, according to what he has done, whether good or bad."*[2] The length of the chronicler's genealogy will fade into insignificance before the list of the redeemed, and alongside each name will be the lifelong record of our conduct and contribution in spiritual service for the King. Not only will we hear His account, we will be accountable: *"So then each of us will give account of himself to God."*[3] It's a sobering thought, isn't it?

Relationships

God's list of names in 1 Chronicles is factual in its responsibilities, and familial in its relationships. It contains ample reference to fathers, sons and brothers, and has a corresponding interest in mothers, wives and sisters. He values each role, and validates them too, so the worldly accuser has no ground on which to accuse Him of being chauvinistic or patronising. Critics have raised their trenchant voices, claiming that the Bible is both, but it is His inspired Word expressing His mind and will, and, since He is neither, it cannot be. He exalts both masculinity and femininity, having created both in mutual perfection, with each equally bearing the image of God and giving glory to Him. Femininity exalts God, but the same cannot be said for feminism. Womanliness is from Him, and women should own His estimation of their womanhood. Feminism is not from Him, and neither is its accompanying claim of women's liberation.

In a similar way, manliness is from Him, and men should own His view of their manhood, but since being patronising toward women is branded as male chauvinism, it also is not of God. Christian men and women are called to be subject, which means that as Christ is never abusive of men who are subject to Him, so men should never abuse women who are subject to Him and to them. Men should honour God by being subject to Him and showing the right attitude to women, and women should honour Him by their subjection, too. Both have a God-given opportunity to magnify Him and the provision of His grace in their subjection, while insubjection in either belongs to personal gratification and the promotion of self.

Character

One of the notable features of Christian homes in northern Myanmar (Burma) is the small noticeboards nailed above each front door. Apart from the name of the family living inside and the church to which they belong, there is a verse of scripture along with a short statement of belief. Some proclaimed, "Jesu in Topa hi" – "Jesus is Lord" – while others said, "Pasian ukna na mang un" – "Obey the will of God." These make a very public declaration, yet it may be in some homes that some of the occupants don't share the faith of their parents. It was a bit like this among the tribes of Israel, too, and this is apparent as we read on through the genealogy.

The named children of Asher were *"heads of their fathers' houses,"* which marked them out as not being mediocre or ordinary, but rather conspicuously at the forefront of family life. In addition to this, they were rated as *"mighty men of valour,"* so they were seen to be strong men who made progress as they championed the cause, and whose virtues were evident. The same was said of the sons of Issachar in chapter 7:2, and of the sons of Benjamin in verse 7, but it was not necessarily an unqualified compliment. This was confirmed in chapter 5:25 after the same two phrases, with the added acclaim of being "famous men," was applied to those from the half-tribe of Manasseh. However, the seeming commendation quickly evaporated when the writer changed course with the condemnation, *"And they were unfaithful to the God of their fathers, and played the harlot after the gods of the peoples of the land."* This was duplicity of the worst kind, done intentionally, and covertly, though they failed to consider that nothing could be covered up before God who sees everything.

It was done as treacherously as Achan's sin in Joshua 7:1 when he stole Jericho's *"accursed things"* and hid them until God exposed his sin with his enforced admission in verse 21, *"I coveted them and took them. And there they are, hidden in the earth in the midst of my tent."* This was the very city Rahab the harlot forsook that she might dwell *"in the midst of Israel,"*[4] yet Achan brought what he could never wear and never spend and kept it "in the midst" of his tent. Have you ever wondered how she felt when the first thing she faced among the people of God was a disappointment? What did she think of a man who couldn't resist keeping something from the place she had so willingly left behind? Under Joshua's leadership, and by the searching work of the Spirit of

95

God, she learned that the people of God couldn't move forward until sin is judged. The same can be said of gatherings of the Lord's people today, that spiritual progress is prevented while there is unjudged sin among them.

A similar question could be asked regarding these unfaithful men from Manasseh, and we can hardly begin to sense the disappointment felt by others, including godly women, when leaders become mis-leaders. Here were men who appeared to be what they were not. Perhaps they impressed others, but not God; they may have been recognised by others, but not by Him. They may have been mighty, valiant, heads and renowned, and some may even have thought them to be 'fit for battle' like the men of Asher, but what good is there in depending upon men who are of some practical use and of no spiritual benefit? Solomon sounded an ever-applicable warning when he said, *"Confidence in an unfaithful man in time of trouble is like a bad tooth and a foot out of joint."*[5] He could hardly have been more graphic for who would trust a broken tooth when chewing or a broken foot for walking? And who would choose to be a victim of such unnecessary hurt? One thing is still evident when we think of Manasseh: there was an essential ingredient missing that made Asher very different in the eyes of God.

Choice men

Suddenly, a new word appears in the vocabulary of the genealogy. It's the word *bᵃrūrīm* from the word *bārar*, which the chronicler would use later in chapters 9:22 and 16:41 to describe those who were *"chosen as gatekeepers"* and *"chosen ... to give thanks to the LORD."* Each of these roles was a distinct honour, and a position of trust, so there must have been good reason for saying they were "chosen." As Levites, the gatekeepers safeguarded the security of the temple and aspects of its sanctity, and we readily understand why it was called *"this trusted office"* in chapter 9:26. As for the singers and musicians, they likewise filled a God-honouring position with their roles being in heartfelt harmony with the offering of the lambs on the altar of burnt offering every morning and evening. In other words, they were the right men for the job and chosen because of their suitability. In a very real way, God was foreshadowing the need for Christlike men to fulfil Christlike ministries.

Each of us has an option: to be famous like the men of Manasseh or choice like those of Asher. However, it's worth keeping in mind that while all famous men are not Christlike, all Christlike men are choice. All this helps to emphasise that God had good reasons for saying the children of Asher were "choice," and the word *bārar* helps us to see what these might be. The Old Testament comes to our aid by the way the same word is translated in other portions of scripture, and they reveal the implications of being "choice":

- 2 Samuel 22:27 - *"With the pure You will show Yourself pure."* Is God choice to me, and am I choice to Him?
- Isaiah 49:2 - *"And He has made My mouth like a sharp sword; In the shadow of His hand He has hidden Me* [kept secret], *and made Me a polished shaft; In His quiver He has hidden Me* [kept close]." Am I allowing God to polish me, that I might become a choice shaft?
- Jeremiah 51:11 - *"Make the arrows bright!"* Is He removing my dullness and making me choice?
- Isaiah 52:11 - *"Depart! Depart! Go out from there, touch no unclean thing; go out from the midst of her, be clean, you who bear the vessels of the LORD."* Am I choice in my separation, so that a holy person can bear holy things?

All these uses of the word can be summed up in the words of Psalm 4:3

— *"But know that the LORD has set apart for Himself him who is godly."* Giving ourselves to godliness will lead to our pureness, brightness, and holiness. God can do nothing with tarnished men who carry excess baggage and, like a rusted arrow, are easily deflected from their course. He looks for men who won't deviate: men of the Word. They are not merely men who want to say something, but men with something to say; not just men who aim to say something, but men who say something with an aim. They are His targeted men who focus on His target. The *"polished shaft"* of Isaiah 49:2 is none other than the Lord Jesus Christ Himself, the One whom God calls *"My Servant"* in verse 3, the Messiah of verse 5 who will *"bring Jacob back to Him,"* and, in verse 6, the *"light to the Gentiles, that* [He] *should be My salvation to the ends of the earth."* He is the co-equal One who reveals the pureness, the brightness, and the holiness of God. He is altogether 'choice,' and the only One through whom God will show Himself "choice" to those who are 'choice'!

And their sister

One of Scripture's lovely examples of togetherness in fellowship is found in Exodus 26:6 — *"And you shall make fifty clasps of gold, and couple the curtains together with the clasps, so that it may be one tabernacle."* It's interesting to note that two of the words used in this verse also appear in 1 Chronicles 7:32. One is taken from the Hebrew word *chābar*, which is translated as 'couple,' and the other from *'achōth*, meaning 'together.' Our verse in 1 Chronicles speaks of Heber whose name comes from *chābar*, his three sons, and of their 'sister,' which is from the word *'achōth*.

Among the initial *"choice men"* of the sons of Asher, God was pleased to mention *"their sister Serah,"* and went on to speak about Heber, his sons, *"and their sister Shua."* We may then wonder if these girls shared their choice character and bore a resemblance to it. They certainly had a God-given opportunity to apply their father's name to their own lives and say, *"I am a companion* [from *chābar*] *of all who fear You, and of those who keep Your precepts."*[6] How wonderful if they truly were included in the *"All these"* in verse 40! Although not included with their brothers as heads, mighty, valiant and chief, there was nothing to prevent them from being pure, bright, polished, clean and choice. Our highest aim is to be choice: not unsuited, not unclean, not unpolished, but coupled together and choice!

While nothing certain is known of these women's achievements, God has recorded their names, and we may take it that fulfilling their meaning would have marked them out as being among those who are choice. Serah means superfluity, as if to suggest an overabundance or excess, and also has the connotation of spreading, like the *"spreading vine"* in Ezekiel 17:6 in its growth and fruitfulness. Just as the words "Heber" and "sister" lead us back to Exodus 26:6, Serah takes us to verse 12 of the same chapter. The associated word *sārach*, with its thought of excess, is associated with the curtains of goats' hair which provided a double pelmet at the front of the Holy Place, and gave an overhang at the back of the Most Holy Place.[7] Young's Literal Translation shows that, being larger, they fulfilled the meaning of the word by protecting the tabernacle curtains underneath. *"And the superfluity in the curtains of the tent — the half of the curtain which is superfluous — hath spread over the hinder part of the tabernacle ... the superfluity in the length of the curtains of the tent, is spread out over the sides."* What a vivid expression of *serach*!

If Serah reflected the character of her brothers, her predecessors and successors, they were suitably complemented in their work for the Lord. This should always be brethren's view of their sisters in the life and work of their assemblies. They are not there only to supplement their brothers, they should have scope to complement them. If they are encouraged to be like Serah, they will automatically be like Shua whose name means 'wealth,' which also is associated with 'freedom,' and we should thank God for sisters who show such abundant riches. Praise God for all whose lives bear testimony of what they are and have in Christ! He has combined the meaning of their names in the riches of His salvation, and His constant assurance is, *"I have come that they may have life, and that they may have it more abundantly."*[8] Yes, He gives it to all who believe, but, sadly, not all show its abundance.

We are living in days when unbelievers reject the gospel and, at the same time, many believers neglect it. For this reason, Hebrews 2:1 says, *"We must give the more earnest heed to the things we have heard."* In an intentional manner, the Inspirer caused the writer to take the character of abundant [*perisson*] life and apply it, not just to giving "heed," but to superabundant heed [*perissoterōs*]. As Ephesians 3:20 so vividly reminds us, it is in His nature to *"do exceedingly abundantly* [*huperekperissou*] *above all that we ask or think,"* and it is within the desire of our new nature that we should *"... abound* [*perisseuō*] *in everything – in faith, in speech, in knowledge, in all diligence, and in your love for us – see that you abound* [*perisseuō*] *in this grace also."*[9] Paul was aware of the Corinthians' reluctance to give to the needy in Jerusalem, and appealed that their abundance of gift would stretch even farther and be seen through grace in the abundance of their giving. All this revolves around the word *perisson*, and there was no doubt they had a superfluity, an excessive amount to give, but it was as if the apostle was asking them to go above and beyond, to *"abound more and more."*[10] In their own way, they showed it's one thing to bear the name "Serah," and quite another to live up to it!

In his commentary on this verse, John MacArthur has written, "Giving does not take place in a vacuum, isolated from other Christian virtues. It must not be done contrary to what is in the heart, for that would be hypocrisy. Paul's affirmation to the Corinthians, you abound in everything (cf. 1 Cor.1:4-7), was an encouraging compliment to those vacillating believers. They abounded in saving, securing, sanctifying faith, having a strong trust in and reliance on the Lord. *Logos* (utterance) refers here not to speech, but to doctrine, 'the word (*logos*) of truth' (2 Cor.6:7; cf. Col.1:5; 2 Tim.2:15; Jas.1:18). Knowledge is the ability to apply doctrine to the issues of life. Earnestness (*spoude*) means 'eagerness,' 'energy,' or 'spiritual passion' (cf. 2 Cor.7:11-12). Love (*agape*) is the noble love of self-sacrifice Paul had inspired in the Corinthians through his example, teaching, and preaching. Because of the spiritual virtues they possessed, Paul exhorted the Corinthians, 'See that you abound in this gracious work also.' God's grace had produced virtues in them, and the apostle wanted it to flow out through their giving" (MacArthur NT Commentary).

Anna ... of the tribe of Asher

How fitting it is that a woman from the tribe of Asher should be linked with the Infant Jesus and celebrated at the opening of the New Testament. The four centuries between the end of Malachi and the birth of Christ are known as the silent years, since there was no written word from God during that period. However, during the final century of that gap, Simeon and Anna were born, and both shared a deep love for God, His Word, and His temple. Anticipating the Messiah, they also shared an understanding of what God would fulfil through Him toward Gentiles and the people of Israel. As Simeon stood with the Saviour in his arms, blessing God and then Joseph and Mary, Anna came with her thanksgiving as she realised that scripture was being fulfilled before her eyes. Like Simeon, who had been *"waiting* [from *prosdechomai*] *for the Consolation of Israel,"*[11] Anna knew that others also *"looked* [from *prosdechomai*] *for redemption in Jerusalem,"*[12] and, being a prophetess, she confidently shared their expectation. Four lovely features of her spirituality are then brought before us to show that she lived a life of faith:

- she did not depart out of the temple;
- she worshipped (RV) with fastings and prayers night and day;
- she gave thanks to God;
- she spoke of Him to all who looked for redemption in Jerusalem.

We can hardly miss the point, that she was a beautiful combination of Serah and Shua's names for she was a woman of true superfluity and wealth. She also, like them, was of the tribe of Asher and "choice." The children of Asher were choice, and children of God should be, too, but the lesson we want to learn from God's summary of them is that His assessment of the men included His acknowledgement of these women. They were not overlooked, and the list would have been poorer without them. Is it not the same today? There is no doubt that God still values choice men and women who give themselves in *"the **will** of God,"*[13] but He longs to see them *"always abounding in the **work** of the Lord."*[14] For this reason, they have equal priority in His eyes in worth and growth, in spirituality and opportunity; and He has said, *"Nevertheless, neither is man independent of woman, nor woman independent of man, in the Lord."*[15] Spiritually, just as naturally, they are mutually indispensable and interdependent. In the same way that Serah and Shua's names added irreplaceable meaning to the names of men belonging to Asher, so godly women today add to the effectiveness of the Lord's people when, by His help, they aim to be choice.

THE POLISHED SHAFT

Not the fame of being famous
Nor the infamy of fame,
But the thought of being faithless (1 Chron.5:23-26)
Gave Manasseh their poor name.
Known as mighty men of valour,
Hailed as heads above their peers,
Yet unfaithfulness had led them
Back to Babylonian spheres.

Not the name of being leaders
Nor the shout of valour's voice,
But the quality of headship
Marked Asher's as being *"choice."* (1 Chron.7:40)
Theirs, a happiness together, (Gen.30:13)
And their character enjoys
Pure and clean and polished brightness:
Features that make God rejoice.

'Neath His shadowed hand is hidden (Isa.49:2)
One He made *"a polished shaft"* –
Brighter far than any arrow
Ever came from archer's craft.
He the Servant and Messiah (Isa.49:5)
Bringing Jacob back to Him,
And a light unto the Gentiles –
Light that never can grow dim!

Man of priceless and peerless worth;
Perfect Servant, perfect Son,
Saviour to the ends of the earth; (Isa.49:6)

Redeemer He, and Holy One. (Isa.49:7)
Pure and unspotted, thus His aim
Never fails to hit the mark.
The *"choice"* One in His Father's Name (Jn 5:43)
Will complete His Father's work. (Jn 10:25)

Chapter 9 Questions

1. What thoughts come into your mind when you think of being at the Judgment seat of Christ, and how do the following verses apply – Romans 14:10, 12; 1 Corinthians 3:13-15; 4:4, 5; and 2 Corinthians 5:10; Revelation 22:12?

2. In what ways are you allowing God to polish you? Are there specific things you would like Him to help you remove, and what do you think He will use to make it happen?

3. How would you help someone who holds feminist views to see that God, the Bible, and Christianity liberate women in the right way?

4. How would you respond to a Christian man who shows signs of being chauvinistic in his attitude to women?

5. What suggestions would you make to help a church address issues such as male chauvinism, feminism, women's liberation and rights, and how can sisters combine with their brethren to present sound biblical perspectives?

6. List the features that, spiritually and practically, contribute to being "choice."

Chapter 10: Building Women

"And next to him was Shallum the son of Hallohesh, leader of half the district of Jerusalem; he and his daughters made repairs" (Neh.3:12).

E ven in spiritual matters, there can be *"A time to break down, and a time to build up."*[1] So it was with the destruction of Jerusalem under Nebuchadnezzar and in its reconstruction under Zerubbabel. In the goodness of God, departure became return, loss turned to recovery, captivity was replaced by freedom, and apathy by revival. Such awakenings are a work of God, and in this case He *"stirred up the spirit of Cyrus king of Persia"*[2] to initiate His people's return and kindle their desire to rebuild.

By doing this, He fulfilled His promise made through Isaiah one hundred and seventy five years earlier regarding Cyrus, *"He is My shepherd, and he shall perform all My pleasure, saying to Jerusalem, 'You shall be built,' and to the temple, 'Your foundation shall be laid.'"*[3] He also proved, as we thought in an earlier chapter, *"The king's heart is in the hand of the LORD, like the rivers of waters; He turns it wherever He wishes."*[4] Such is His power through every instrument that fulfils His purpose!

God everywhere hath sway,
And all things serve His might;
His every act pure blessing is,
His path unsullied light.
He hath made bare His arm,
Who shall His work withstand?

'Tis He His people's cause defends,
Who then shall stay His hand?
We comprehend Him not;
Yet earth and heaven tell,
God sits as Sovereign on the throne,
And ruleth all things well.
(Trans. By J. Wesley from P. Gerhardt)

Babylon had been a song-less place, and we sense the anguish and pain of the people's seventy years lost from their homeland and from the city of the great King. Psalm 137 captures their grief:

"By the rivers of Babylon,
There we sat down, yea, we wept
When we remembered Zion.
We hung our harps
Upon the willows in the midst of it.
For there those who carried us away captive asked of us a song,
And those who plundered us requested mirth,
Saying, 'Sing us one of the songs of Zion!'
How shall we sing the LORD's song
In a foreign land?
If I forget you, O Jerusalem,
Let my right hand forget its skill!

> *If I do not remember you,*
> *Let my tongue cling to the roof of my mouth—*
> *If I do not exalt Jerusalem*
> *Above my chief joy."*

In contrast, how fitting is the jubilation of Psalm 126!

> *"When the LORD brought back the captivity of Zion,*
> *We were like those who dream.*
> *Then our mouth was filled with laughter,*
> *And our tongue with singing.*
> *Then they said among the nations,*
> *'The LORD has done great things for them.'*
> *The LORD has done great things for us,*
> *And we are glad."*

What a change from the groaning of Babylon, to anticipating the glory of Jerusalem! However, just as the Song of Moses was replaced by complaining at Marah in Exodus 15, and the Song of Deborah's triumph in Judges 5 faded into defeat in chapter 6, so the height of joy and singing of the returning captives turned to depths of despair and sighing in Jerusalem. The words of Psalm 102:13 and 14 would become true, but discovering their truth would come with much effort.

> *"You will arise and have mercy on Zion;*
> *For the time to favour her,*
> *Yes, the set time, has come.*
> *For Your servants take pleasure in her stones,*
> *And show favor to her dust [from ʿāphār]."*

Everyone to his work – 4:15

When a work of God is begun, the adversary will have new enemies ready to appear on the doorstep, and it wasn't long until Nehemiah knew that Sanballat and Tobiah *"were deeply disturbed that a man had come to seek the well-being of the children of Israel."*[5] They thought little of the people who had come to Zion as singers, but were more outraged that they had returned as workers. Nor did they hold back from mocking them: *"What are these feeble Jews doing? Will they fortify themselves? Will they offer sacrifices? Will they complete it in a day? Will they revive the stones from the heaps of rubbish* [from *'āphār*]—*stones that are burned?"*[6] Initially, the people of God wavered and admitted, *"The strength of the laborers is failing, and there is so much rubbish* [from *'āphār*] *that we are not able to build the wall."*[7]

This was a lot to acknowledge for it meant they felt differently within themselves and toward the heaps that lay at their feet. It also meant the inner conviction of being overcomers had faded and had to be regained through prayer and Nehemiah's encouragement. While facing the threat of being under attack, they turned to God – *"Nevertheless we made our prayer to our God, and because of them we set a watch against them day and night."*[8] They needed to recapture the vision as builders who took pleasure in her stones, and showed favour to her dust. Having done this, Nehemiah says, *"all of us returned to the wall, everyone to his work."*[9] Just like today, there was no reason for anyone to feel they couldn't be included or that doing their bit was optional. Alas, some did!

* Their nobles did not put their shoulders to the work

This is one part of Scripture where 'everyone' clearly doesn't mean everyone, and Nehemiah was very much aware of it. His list of builders in chapter 3 His appreciation of the Tekoites was real: mentioning, first of all, that they *"made repairs,"* before adding they *"repaired another section."*[10] However, one thing detracted from their zeal: their nobles had none and *"did not put their shoulders* [from *tsavvār* – necks] *to the work of their LORD."*

What hindered them? Was it the unavoidable practicality of getting dirty or was it the unavailable spirituality that left them unwilling to make the sacrifice? The first certainly was a definite part of a builder's commitment, and Nehemiah drew attention to the fact that, *"Neither I, my brethren, my servants, nor the men of the guard who followed me took off our clothes, except that everyone took them off for washing."*[11] Whatever their reason, they deprived themselves of the initial satisfaction of rebuilding for God and of ever being able to see where they had done their bit for Him.

As we think of their reluctance, may we never imitate their lack of willingness or conclude that some sacrifices are too big to make. It may be that we rule ourselves out because the particular work is "Not for me!" or that we don't want to devote so much effort or time to His service. The nobles missed out because they didn't put their shoulders to the work for fifty-two days[12] to building the wall. Will we, likewise, miss out by putting time constraints on what we do for the Lord? May God keep us from losing the sense of sacrifice that makes His service so much more honouring to Him and fulfilling to us. How easy it is to sing, "All to Jesus I surrender," and then hold back from giving more of ourselves or more of our time because of personal or family constraints!

Keil and Delitzsch make this comment. "The expression 'to bring the neck to service' is, according to Jeremiah 27:11 – *"But the nations that brings their necks under the yoke"* – to be understood as meaning: to bring the neck under the yoke of any one, i.e. to subject oneself to another … It is questionable whether *'ªdonēyhem* is to be taken as the plural of excellence, and understood as God, [as in Deut.10:17; Ps.135:5; Mal.1:6]; or of earthly lords or rulers [as in Gen.40:1; 2 Sam.10:3; 1 Kin.12:27]. The former view seems to be decidedly correct, for it cannot be discerned how the suffix should … prevent our thinking of the service of God, if the repairing of the wall of Jerusalem may be regarded as a service required by God and rendered to Him. Besides, the fact that *'ªdōnīm* is only used of kings, and is inapplicable whether to authorities in Jerusalem or to Nehemiah, speaks against referring it to secular rulers or authorities" (Keil & Delitzsch Commentary on the Old Testament).

This raises a question that is as appropriate now as it was then: if it was the work of their Lord, why were they absent instead of being involved, and why were they not actively under His lordship? First of all, they were defective in their submission to Him; secondly, they were ineffective by not having communion with their brethren. This left them open to justifiable criticism: that they dishonoured the Lord and could have discouraged their brethren.

Sadly, the writer of Hebrews was concerned about a similar omission among early Christians and warned them about *"not forsaking the assembling of ourselves together, as is the manner of some."*[13] We ought to have the reality of His lordship **behind** us in the promise of our salvation, *"if you confess with your mouth that Jesus is Lord and believe in your heart that God raised Him from the dead, you will be saved."*[14] Likewise, we have the assurance of His lordship **beside** us daily in our progress as we *"grow in the grace and knowledge of our Lord and Saviour Jesus Christ."*[15]

And we have this prospect **before** us, as we are urged to *"be even more diligent to make your call and election sure, for if your do these things you will never stumble; for so an entrance will be supplied to you abundantly into the everlasting kingdom of our Lord and Saviour Jesus Christ."*[16]

Next

This was another aspect in which the nobles failed to share for building a wall makes the word *"next"* a conjunction in more ways than one. Nehemiah 3 stands as a record to fellowship in building, and each *"next"* introduces the successive bond that allowed the wall to become one. It demands a company of constructive workers whose work blends with each other's, and the nobles missed out in the great succession of being *"next."*

* Goldsmiths, perfumers, merchants – vv.8,31,32

Among those who gave themselves to the work on Jerusalem's wall were goldsmiths who left their work with gold to take pleasure in her stones. They, normally, would have treasured every glint of precious gold dust, but now they showed favour to her dust while discarding it as they recovered stones from among the rubble.

Next to them was one of the perfumers whose hands would have been accustomed to mixing spices and other ingredients for fragrant ointments. The *"art of the perfumer"* was highly regarded among the people of God from the days of Exodus 30:25 and 35 when the holy anointing oil and incense were in their safekeeping. Its fragrance was kept for permeating the tabernacle, the high priest and the priests, and the incense filled the atmosphere of the Holy Place as it burned on the golden altar. Now, on the wall, a perfumer worked alongside a goldsmith complementing one another, while God saw glory and fragrance working together in the very different atmosphere of a building site. Merchants also joined with goldsmiths in the varied workforce that concluded at the Sheep Gate where Eliashib the high priest had begun.

It was a unified and unifying work, lessons from which come down the centuries to emphasise that the work of the Lord always is. The most gifted specialist can join with others who could never be linked with them in their daily occupation, just as the academic can be harnessed with those who are not so literate in a gathering of the Lord's people. Work on the wall proved that it was the similarity of the building, the beams and bolts and bars that mattered, and not the differences in the types of worker.

* Shallum ... and his daughters – v.12

Among all the men that enlisted as builders, God noted a group of daughters who worked alongside their father, perhaps in the absence of any brothers. Their grandfather was Hallohesh whose name has different connotations, but comes from *lachash*, which means 'a whisper.' Isaiah used it very meaningfully in chapter 26:16 (NIV), *"LORD, they came to you in their distress; when you disciplined them, they could barely whisper a prayer."* Albert Barnes comments in his notes, "The Hebrew word *lachash* means properly a whispering, muttering; and through a sighing, a calling for help. This is the sense here. In their calamity they sighed, and called on God for help." Perhaps, Hallohesh did the same while in the hardship of Babylonian captivity and left a godly imprint in his son, Shallum, and his granddaughters. If so, his whispers in Babylon were followed by their singing on their way back to Jerusalem and, finally, by their working on the wall. Their togetherness marked the goodness of

God to their father whose name, Shallum, means 'reward.' As fellow-labourers they shared the recompense that only God can give in the way that Boaz promised Ruth, *"The LORD repay [from shālam] your work, and a full reward be given you by the LORD God of Israel, under whose wings you have come for refuge."*[17]

In recognising these daughters for their work, God included them among all who *"made repairs"* as, around forty times, each and every one drew on the word *chāzaq* to strengthen the city's wall and gates. Unlike the nobles whose absence is noted by one verse in God's Word, so these dear women's presence is given a verse that records their input to a vital work for God.

Time and again in the New Testament, the call for strengthening was given. As the Lord anticipated Peter's recovery from denying Him, He urged him, *"strengthen [from stērizō] your brethren."*[18] Later, Judas and Silas went to Antioch where they *"exhorted and strengthened [from stērizō] the brethren with many words."*[19] As the Lord walked in the midst of the lampstands that represented the seven churches in Asia, He called for Sardis to *"strengthen the things that remain."*[20] However, before we can impart strength to anyone, we need to be strengthened ourselves; and before there can be a work of God through us, there needs to be a work of God in us. To be able, we need to be enabled, and for this reason *"The God of all grace, who called you to his eternal glory in Christ, after you have suffered a little, will himself restore [from katartizō, repair] you and make you strong [from sterizō], firm and steadfast."*[21] Just as Shallum and his daughters needed their lives repaired and strengthened before setting out from Babylon to repair and strengthen things in Jerusalem, so we need to be spiritually repaired and strengthened before we can be used by God to do it for others.

Bring the Book – 8:1-12

We learn from Nehemiah 6:15 that the wall was finished on the twenty-fifth day of Elul, which was the sixth month of the Jewish year. Five days later, on the first day of the seventh month, and standing with the newly built wall as their background—

> *"the people gathered together as one man … and they told Ezra the scribe to bring the Book of the Law of Moses … And Ezra opened the book in the sight of all the people, for he was standing above all the people and when he opened it, all the people stood up … And they bowed their heads and worshiped the LORD with their faces to the ground."*

What a commendable desire and reverence for the Word of God! They were so moved that Nehemiah told them, *"This day is holy to the LORD your God; do not mourn or weep." For all the people wept, when they heard the words of the Law."* Then he added, *"Do not sorrow, for the joy of the LORD is your strength."* This was the remarkable result of their equally remarkable request: *"Bring the Book,"* and we would do well to see the connection that all builders need the Book. Being moved by the Word, belongs to feeling its impact through the attention of the mind and the affection of the heart. Our English Bibles combine these by saying that *"the ears of all the people were attentive,"*[22] and *"all the people wept."*[23] Among them were the goldsmiths, perfumers, merchants, Shallum's daughters, and every builder. All of them were affected in the same way: in tears from one morning spent in the Book, and discovering that they needed the Book if the joy of the LORD was to be their strength.

Is it not the same for us? Our joy and strength are dependent on the Book. Its place in our lives and in the churches will always determine the level of our joy and strength. It's our only means of strengthening the things that remain and, if its presence ensures that the joy of the Lord is our strength, its absence will lead to lack of joy becoming our weakness. Paul could recall his three years of preaching in Ephesus being *"night and day with tears,"*[24] and that he thought of Timothy *"night and day ... being mindful of your tears."*[25] Some think Timothy's tears were shed when Paul left the Ephesians in Acts 20:36-38, but it may be more than this, as suggested by Dr. H. A. Ironside — "Evidently Timothy was very tender-hearted and affectionate and wept over sinners and over his own sins." Adam Clarke also widens the possibility by saying, "Whether the apostle refers to the affecting parting with the Ephesian church, or to the deep impressions made on Timothy's heart when he instructed him in the doctrine of Christ crucified ... it is not certainly known."

When last were you moved by a preacher who wept as he preached the Word? And when last were you so moved by the Word that you wept? We do know that both of these great men of God shed tears. We also know of the woman who was so moved that she *"washed His* [Jesus'] *feet with her tears and wiped them with the hair of her head."*[26] She was so moved that she brought her grief and her glory to His feet, and there's no higher place for any woman, or any man, to be!

Chapter 10 Questions

1. In what ways is the lordship of Christ being effective in your own life, as you enjoy the truth of it: a) Behind you in the promise of your salvation (Rom.10:9; Col.2:6,7)? b) Beside you in the progress of your daily walk (Eph.4:1; 5:2,8,15; Col.3:24; 2 Pet.3:18)? c) Before you in the prospect of being ready for His coming (2 Thess.2:13-17; 2 Pet.1:11)?

2. As we combine the prayers of Hallohesh with the reward of Shallum and his daughters as fellow-workers, how do these thoughts come together to help us *"strengthen the things that remain"* (Rev.3:2; Lk.22:32; Jude 20,21)?

3. As we think of *"next"* and *"everyone to his work"* (4:15), what help can be given to encourage everyone to fulfil a role in their local church, so that everyone becomes a builder in one way or another?

Chapter 11: The Woman at the Well

"He left Judea and departed again to Galilee. But He needed to go through Samaria. So He came to a city of Samaria which is called Sychar, near the plot of ground that Jacob gave to his son Joseph. Now Jacob's well was there. Jesus therefore, being from His journey, sat thus by the well. It was about the sixth hour. A woman of Samaria came to draw water. Jesus said to her, 'Give Me a drink.' For His disciples had gone away into the city to buy food. Then the woman of Samaria said to Him, 'How is it that You, being a Jew, ask a drink from me, a Samaritan woman?' For Jews have no dealings with Samaritans. Jesus answered and said to her, 'If you knew the gift of God, and who it is who says to you, "Give Me a drink," you would have asked Him, and He would have given you living water.' 'Are You greater than our father Jacob? Sir, I perceive that You are a prophet. I know that Messiah is coming (who is called Christ)"' (Jn 4:3-10,12,19,25).

Who would have thought that among the wreckage of this woman's life a seed of hope nestled in her mind waiting for the Author of Life[1] to germinate it? He had proved Himself to be the Restorer of a religious wreck in the privacy of nighttime in John 3, in daytime for this moral wreck in chapter 4, and would again in the openness of a poolside for a physical wreck in John 5.

John gives another lovely connection, by helping us to see water-carriers in chapter 2 who became wine-waiters when Jesus changed water into wine, then He Himself carried the message of being *"born of water"* to Nicodemus in chapter 3, and now waits to meet the water-carrier at Sychar in chapter 4. Mary's comment in chapter 2:5 could have been brought forward as good advice to the woman: *"Whatever He says to you, do it."* The Lord's words in chapter 3:20 could have been applied to her, too: *"For everyone practicing evil hates the light and does not come to the light, lest their* [her] *deeds should be exposed."* But, this time, His approach would not be by command or by warning, but by request. This in itself would shock the woman for, normally, Jewish men would ignore women in public, and coming alone may also indicate that she avoided the tongues of other well-bound women who would have known her background.

We know nothing of what reverie occupied that mind as she made her way to the well. Perhaps, like a becalmed sea, nothing stirred, but it was about to change. Unbeknown to her, the Man she could see at her well had chosen one of three routes to Galilee that He might meet her there to turn the tide of her thinking and behaviour. Four waves of interest began to lap, each one bringing her nearer to the safety of a haven she never knew existed. Beginning with what she knew, He graciously led her to discover what she didn't know. One thing we will learn about her is, she was a thinker.

"How is it that You, being a Jew?" – v.9

As to His nationality, she was right. He was part Jew, because He was the *"Child"*[2] who was *"born"*[2] of an earthly mother. What she didn't know was that He is the *"Son"*[2] who was *"given"*[2] by His heavenly Father. She saw Him as a Man, because He is the last Adam in His humanity; and as a Jew, because of His nationality. By seeing Him as a Jew, her Samaritan mind would have concluded that He would have *"no dealings"* with her and therefore wouldn't ask, *"Give Me a drink."* The word *synchrōntai* helps us to understand why she couldn't grasp that He, as a Jew, would even ask her to let Him drink from her waterpot, since no Jew would expect a favour from a Samaritan. Practically speaking, it implies they had nothing in common to speak about and no expectation of sharing anything together. But He wasn't there to deal with her as a Jew: as God manifested in the flesh, He was there to reveal favour from the heart of God by reaching hers. Through grace, He had overcome the first barrier by communicating, and God was speaking in His Son.

"Are You greater than our father Jacob?" – v.12

Again, she was right: this time, because of His superiority. What she didn't know was that she was speaking with the One who is co-equal with the Father and the Holy Spirit as *"The God of Abraham, Isaac, and Jacob,"*[3] who also was able to say, *"Before Abraham was, I AM."*[4] To help her toward this He prompted her to think of the nature of the gift of God, and what it is; the nature of the Speaker, and who He is; the nature of the living water He offered, and how to get it. Instead she reverted to what she thought she knew by pointing out that He had *"nothing to draw with,"* yet He was gradually drawing her! She had come to draw, but was being drawn. In His eyes, she was the one with nothing to draw. She could draw Sychar's water up, but couldn't draw the Saviour's living water down.

Secondly, her claim to having Jacob as father wasn't altogether true. National tendencies are sometimes as pronounced as personal traits, and national features can be as recognisable as family likenesses. Whether in looks, language or lifestyle, likenesses can be hard to overcome. The seeds of the woman's situation were sown far back in history, mired in a foreign land among false gods when the Assyrians took Israel into captivity in 2 Kings 17. Samaritans became a mixed race after the area was repopulated in 2 Kings 17:24 when *"The king of Assyria brought people from Babylon ... and placed them in the cities of Samaria instead of the children of Israel; and they took possession of Samaria and dwelt in its cities."*

Rather than pursue her diversions, the Lord drew a different kind of response by assuring her that He had water that would overcome her thirst forever, since it would become an inner fountain *"springing up into everlasting life."* This was of immediate interest and she voiced its convenience – *"Sir, give me this water, that I may not thirst, nor come here to draw,"* – but He came straight to the point that this water is received, not for convenience, but through conviction. In His own patient way, He changed from wanting to be the Drinker to being the Giver, and she changed from being the giver to wanting to be the drinker!

"Sir, I perceive that You are a prophet" – v.19

For the third time, she was right, because of His authenticity. Unlike all earlier prophets, He had not come to reveal something from God, but as the complete revelation of God. They shared something of His purpose and revealed it to those who were *"willing and obedient."*[5] He shared the entirety of His Person and reveals it to whom *"[He] wills to reveal*

Him."[6] She knew in part, because Moses had spoken about One of whom God had said, *"I will raise up for them a Prophet like you from among their brethren, and will put My words in His mouth, and He shall speak to them all that I command Him."*[7] What she didn't yet know was that right before her sat the promised Prophet, His Servant Jesus, whom God had sent *"to bless* [her]*, in turning* [her] *away from* [her] *iniquities."*[8]

Initially, His request, *"Go, call your husband, and come here,"* seemed straightforward and easily sidestepped, but her denial led the Lord to expose the sordid state of her life. Suddenly, her perception of Him changed. She no longer thought of Him as a Jew or as being greater than Jacob, but as a prophet. He had touched a raw nerve, and she felt uncomfortable. The One who searches hearts[9] was searching hers, and calling her to search it too. He was *"wearied from His journey,"* and knew it; she should have been wearied by her life's journey, but didn't know it. Nor did she know how far He had come or how far He would go: from Judea, from heaven, from the Father for her, for the cross, and for the throne.

He had come to call those *"who labour and are heavy laden,"*[10] and she would never know the blessing of His rest until she knew the burden of her sin. She couldn't know the comfort of His gift without being made uncomfortable about her guilt. She couldn't know the peace of God's forgiveness without being troubled by her sinfulness. He knew she was cohabiting with a man who was not her husband, and wanted her to know that sinful living and living water never cohabit. He was the light, and she was in darkness, and these also don't cohabit. He was calling her to *"turn ... from darkness to light, and from the power of Satan to God, that you* [she] *may receive forgiveness of sins."*[11]

What wonderful power lies in the gospel of Christ! Through it, He causes sinners to turn. Therefore God's gospel appeal is, *"Repent therefore, and turn back, that your sins may be blotted out, that times of refreshing may come from the presence of the Lord."*[12] He also assures us that, through redemption and forgiveness, *"He has delivered us from the power of darkness and conveyed us into the kingdom of the Son of His love."*[13] Grace, through the goodness of God,[14] gives the power to repent and turn. God has the power to blot out and deliver. In this glorious freedom, we don't retain the sinful lifestyle of which we have repented,[15] or return to the sin from which we have turned away. Neither will God lose those whom He saves or disown those He has delivered.[16] But what do we know about *"times of refreshing"*? There are many ways by which the Lord refreshes His people, and He instantly spoke of one as soon as the woman mentioned worship.

"I know that Messiah is coming" – v.25

So far, the Lord had revealed quite a bit to her. Firstly, in letting her see that He regarded no barrier between Jew and Samaritan, just as would be removed between Jew and Gentile through His blood.[17] Next, He introduced her to thoughts of the gift of God, of Himself, and of living water. Then He challenged her sinful ways before revealing to her that Gerizim and Jerusalem would no longer be places of worship. He had something better to tell her: *"The hour is coming, and now is, when the true worshipers will worship the Father in spirit and truth, for the Father is seeking such to worship Him."* How privileged she was, that His purpose in travelling through Samaria was not only to meet her, but to make her the vessel of such blessing. We can imagine her eyes widening in wonder as He pointed inward to her coming as a sinner and then forward to the prospect of coming among worshippers.

As she took it all in, she saw beyond the Jew, and Jacob, and a prophet, and was able to say, *"I know that Messiah is coming."* In response, Jesus answered, *"I who speak to you am He,"* or as a direct translation from Greek says, "I am that speak to you." For the first time in John's Gospel, He shared His eternal and ever-present name – *Egō eimi* – and made Himself known to her as the I AM. Step by step, He had taken her thoughts beyond His humanity as a man, His nationality as a Jew, His superiority as greater than Jacob, and His authenticity as the Prophet, to His Deity as the Messiah. He never asked her name – though He could have done for, like the doorkeeper in John 10:3, He calls His sheep by name – but He told her His name.

Is it important to know His name? Yes, absolutely, for Jesus said, *"If you do not believe that I am [Egō eimi] He, you will die in your sins."*[18] Samaritans would know from the Torah, the first five books of the Bible, that "I AM" is the name by which God revealed Himself to Moses in Exodus 3:14, but the woman was yet to discover that this name also belongs to the Man who spoke with her.

John records in chapter 1:41 that Andrew was the first among Jews to say, *"We have found the Messiah,"* and the woman was first among Samaritans to go to others with the question, *"Come, see a Man who told me all things that I ever did. Could this be the Christ?"* In her rush to go and tell, *"she left her waterpot,"* and this wasn't inadvertent for she intended coming back. In her newfound spirit of evangelism, and like a vessel filled to the brim, she went into the city to pour out her story. She left the well and went home with the fountain, and fully aware that He was much more interested in her as a vessel than in her waterpot. She had begun the day, in her old lifestyle of leading men astray. It ended in a new lifestyle of leading men to Christ. Presumably, her live-in partner was at her side. The beauty of her testimony was that she brought them to see Christ for who He said He is, and not for who she thought Him to be: not to her measurable view of Him in relation to the Jew or Jacob or prophets, but to the immeasurable Christ of God.

Knowing about a well whose history went back to Genesis, she would be familiar with the others that were dug in the days of Abraham and Isaac. On reflection, she may even have entered into the meaning of their names.

- Esek got its name from the quarrelling that took place between the herdsmen of Gerar and Isaac's herdsmen, and so it commemorated the strife that took place among them (Gen.26:20);
- Sitnah's name was given for the self-same reason, as a constant reminder of the opposition and resistance that was experienced there (Gen.26:21);
- Rehoboth was different, and with a sense of relief Isaac said, *"Now the LORD has made room for us, and we shall be fruitful in the land"* (Gen.26:22);
- Shebah at Beersheba was linked to the thought of 'The well of the oath' (Gen.21:31; 26:33).

Each of these could have been a voice to her. Perhaps, like Esek, she recognised her initial non-compliant reaction to the Man who humbled Himself to speak to her. Was there not also evidence of Sitnah in the resistance she showed toward Him? Even so, she would forever recall how He wrote 'Rehoboth' over their conversation, that she also might say, "The LORD has made room for me." And, by His grace, did it not also become her Beersheba, since He made it the well of the oath for her?

All these could be so fittingly applied to her, but how could she miss the similarity between her and Rebekah, the other water-carrier of Genesis

24? Her experience of being called to Isaac's side began at a well, and her arrival in his presence was marked by his coming from Beer Lahai Roi. Could Sychar's woman not borrow its meaning and always look at her landmark as "The well of the Living One who sees me"?

Two different words are used for the well in John 4. Twice in verse 6, in relation to the Lord, it is called '*pēgē*'; and twice in verses 11 and 12, in relation to the woman, it is called '*phrear.*' The first refers to a gushing fountain or spring, the second to a hole or a pit that has been dug for obtaining or holding water. As soon as she had spoken of its depth and origin, Jesus continued to tell her about the water He could give. Significantly, verse 14 uses the word again to describe how it *"will become in* him [her] *a fountain [pēgē] of water springing up into everlasting life."* Having heard her description of the well, He returned to describing His gift as a lively fountain and didn't resort to whatever she had said in her language. The great thing is He never came down to her word, but brought her up to His!

Thankfully, He has drawn us as He drew her, and calls us to show that we are blessed through the indwelling Spirit, as we read in John 7:37-39, with an inner gushing fountain that no other well can supply: *"On the last day, that great day of the feast, Jesus stood and cried out, saying, 'If anyone thirsts, let him come to Me and drink. He who believes in Me, as the Scripture has said, out of his heart will flow rivers of living water.' But this He spoke concerning the Spirit, whom those believing in Him would receive; for the Holy Spirit was not yet given, because Jesus was not yet glorified."* Like Psalm 87:7, we can say to Him, *"All my springs are in you."*

> Little thought Samaria's daughter
> On that ne'er forgotten day
> That the tender Shepherd sought her

126

As a sheep astray
That from sin He longed to win her
Knowing more than she could tell
Of the wretchedness within her
Waiting at the well.
Neath the stately palm tree swaying
Listened she to words of truth
While each thought was backward straying
O'er her wasted youth.
Hast'ning homeward with desire
All His wondrous speech to tell
Asked she, "Is not the Messiah
Waiting at the well?"
Yet salvation's well is flowing,
And the Saviour listens there
Ev'ry want and care foreknowing,
To our humble prayer.
By his gracious smile of favour
While our hearts with rapture swell,
Well we know it is the Saviour
Waiting at the well.
Living waters still are flowing,
Full and free for all mankind,
Blessings sweet on all bestowing—
All may welcome find.
All the world may come and prove Him,
Every doubt will Christ dispel;
And each heart shall truly love Him,
Waiting at the well.
(Sophia T. Griswold)

Chapter 11 Questions

1. How would you help someone who didn't understand the gospel to think about the nature of the gift of God, the nature of the Lord Jesus as Saviour, and the nature of the living water He provides?
2. God's desire for worship may not be part of our gospel witness, yet Jesus included it and made this woman highly privileged by revealing it to her. How can we link the salvation for sinners with the call to be worshippers?
3. She also was the first person in John's Gospel to whom Jesus introduced Himself as the "I AM" (6:35; 8:12; 10:7; 10:11; 11:25; 14:6; 15:1). How does it give meaning to each statement?
4. As a lesson in witnessing, the Lord gave the woman valuable details of the gospel by revealing: a) the need to overcome a barrier b) the gift of living water c) dealing with sin, d) worship and e) Himself as the I AM. How can we follow the importance of weaving these into the way we witness?

Chapter 12: An Infirm Woman

"Now He was teaching in one of the synagogues on the Sabbath. And behold, there was a woman who had a spirit of infirmity eighteen years, and was bent over and could in no way raise herself up. But when Jesus saw her, He called her to Him and said to her, 'Woman, you are loosed from your infirmity.' And He laid His hands on her, and immediately she was made straight, and glorified God. But the ruler of the synagogue answered with indignation, because Jesus had healed on the Sabbath; and he said to the crowd, 'There are six days on which men ought to work; therefore come and be healed on them, and not on the Sabbath day.' The Lord then answered him and said, 'Hypocrite! Does not each one of you on the Sabbath loose his ox or donkey from the stall, and lead it away to water it? So ought not this woman, being a daughter of Abraham, whom Satan has bound—think of it—for eighteen years, be loosed from this bond on the Sabbath?' And when He said these things, all His adversaries were put to shame; and all the multitude rejoiced for all the glorious things that were done by Him" (Lk.13:10-17).

T he Lord's miracles were not random, unconnected events that took place without relevance to His teaching. An example of this is seen in Matthew 16:5-12 when the disciples misunderstood the Lord's remark about *"the leaven of the Pharisees and the Sadducees."* Assuming He was pointing out that they had forgotten to bring bread, they were challenged regarding what they had witnessed in the feeding of the five thousand among Jews or the four thousand among Gentiles. Instead, He meant the hypocrisy that permeated the pernicious teaching of these ungodly Pharisees and Sadducees in contrast to what He taught. The contrast is seen in their demand for a sign in verse 1, while His aim in the chapter was to speak to His disciples of His Deity in verses 13-17, His church in verse 18, His death and resurrection in verses 21-23, and His future glory in verse 28. The Pharisees and Sadducees were so blind they couldn't see the first of these – the Son as the best Sign from heaven as God manifested in the flesh – and therefore could never see the others.

The blind man in John 9 was illustrative of the blindness of Israel in Romans 11:25, which says, *"blindness in part has happened to Israel."* in saying this, Paul doesn't mean that partial blindness has gripped the nation, rather that total blindness has gripped part of the nation. In the mercy of God, many Jews are being turned to Christ through the gospel, and, in a day still to come, "[God] *will pour on the house of David and on the inhabitants of Jerusalem the Spirit of grace and supplication; then they will look on Me whom they pierced."*[1] The deaf and mute in Mark 7:37 also symbolised a nation that wouldn't hear or speak of Him, though the day will come for the remnant of Israel when *"The lame shall leap like a deer, and the tongue of the dumb sing."*[2]

When we come to Luke 13, the barren fig tree is symbolic of Israel's fruitlessness, and, significantly, it is at this point Luke introduces the woman who has been bent over for eighteen years. That she came to the synagogue on the day Jesus was teaching, is testimony to His omniscience. He knew she would be there, and that is testimony to her faithfulness. In spite of the inconvenience of each agonising step, and discomfort along with the shame of her disability, she was drawn to where she would hear the Scriptures read, not knowing she was about to see and meet and be touched by the Word Himself.

Being there was no accident, for her meeting with Him was by perfect divine timing, like Zacchaeus in Luke 19:1-10, and Simon of Cyrene in Mark 15:21. It was their final opportunity for Jesus was passing through Jericho for the last time when He called on Zacchaeus, and going out of Jerusalem for the last time on His way to Golgotha when Simon was compelled to bear His cross. As for the woman, it was probably the Lord's final visit to a synagogue. There is no mention of what He was teaching and, unlike the woman at the well, there was no input from her. His whole focus was to teach and challenge by the miraculous means of healing what was so evidently wrong with her.

And behold, there was a woman

Like theirs, our attention is drawn to her and to her condition, and we recognise she was completely bowed and powerless to unbend herself. As her body language filled their eyes, the laboured shuffling of her feet filled their ears. Undoubtedly, His day had begun like every other in communion with His Father, sharing how He would *"speak a word in season to him* [her] *who is weary."*[3] Having come for her sake, He saw her with the compassion of the One *"Who dwells on high, Who humbles Himself to behold the things that are in the heavens and in the earth? He raises the poor out of the dust, and lifts* [up] *the needy."*[4] And well might she have borrowed Job's words, *"Does He not see my ways, and count all my steps?"*[5]

One renowned Christian surgeon has said she "was suffering from spondylitis deformans; the bones of her spine were fused into a rigid mass" (Modern Discovery and the Bible by A. Rendle Short, M.D., B.S., B.Sc., F.R.C.S.). She was stooped and bound, and knew it, but the Lord knew she was surrounded by others whose minds and hearts were spiritually crippled, and they didn't know it. Her vision was fixed downward, and, in a different sense, so was theirs. She must have longed to be upright, while they, believing themselves to be upright, saw no such need. Bodily, she was far from straight, but her heart was, and well might she have said, like David in Psalm 7:10, *"My defense is of God, who saves the upright* [from *yāshār* – straight] *in heart."* She probably pleaded often with Him about her physical condition, and He could have assured her through Proverbs 15:8 that *"the prayer of the upright is His delight."*

Knowing all their hearts, Jesus called the woman and, as His invitation rang out in the synagogue, He demonstrated what He taught in Matthew 9:12 and 13 — *"Those who are well have no need of a physician, but those who are sick. But go and learn what this means: 'I desire mercy and not sacrifice.' For I did not come to call the righteous, but sinners, to repentance."* In a rather dramatic manner He diverted their eyes from Himself and their ears from His ministry to concentrate on her, because she was there in the purpose of God and not by accident. Like the feeding of the five thousand, when *"He Himself knew what He would do,"*[6] He was about to meet her need, cure her ailment, cancel her limitations, increase her awareness of divine power, and give her a future.

Woman, you are loosed

It was a life-changing call and, having come forward at His request, His statement further divided the gathering: *"Woman, you are loosed from your infirmity."* He saw, He called, He spoke, He touched, and He healed. Holiness confronted hopelessness, Omnipotence overcame impotence, liberty replaced bondage, His touch conquered deformity, and His command defeated the Adversary. Since she was now so near to Him, *"He laid His hands on her, and immediately she was made straight, and glorified God."* From being stooped, she became upright; from being bound, she was freed; from being ill, she became well; and from being silent, she became vocal. Physically, she responded to His word, and she stood erect for the first time in eighteen years.

She also responded spiritually to show that His healing word found responsive faith in her, but we can borrow the words of Hebrews 4:2 and apply them to the ruler of the synagogue and the crowd: *"but the word which they heard did not profit them, not being mixed with faith in those who heard it."* Spiritual profit always expresses itself, and the woman spontaneously magnified God. She had been so stooped, her face was near the level of the feet of Him who *"made the stars also,"*[7] and that night she would be able to see them as she had never done in eighteen years.

From a spiritual point of view, there may be times when we say with David in Psalm 145:14, *"The LORD ... raises up all who are bowed down."* The language here is very reminiscent of how the woman looked, which no one could fail to see, but David was speaking about something very different. Sometimes burdens that are not seen by others and not known to them, weigh so heavily that spirits droop and believers sag under trials that become spiritually backbreaking. There is a danger that such struggles go unnoticed by others and we become fettered by thoughts that take us on a gradual downward curve. The Adversary will do his utmost to hijack our attitudes and actions, to the extent that churches can be unsettled when saints struggle with problems that are unresolved and not straightened out. It is then that we feel so thankful for this assurance, the LORD *"upholds."* The word of His grace comes to our aid, as He causes us to rest on the comfort of His promises to prop up tired minds and weary hearts, and those who are *"bowed"* are strengthened by His timely support and kept from collapse.

The woman must have rejoiced in His omnipotence that had brought immediate liberty and release from her body's formerly locked position. She also would have realised that a battle had just been won, in that, having been bound by Satan, he had been overcome by a work of God and she was free. She must also have wondered about His omniscience for how could He have claimed her as *"a daughter of Abraham"* in recognition of her faith, just as He referred to Zacchaeus as *"a son of Abraham."*[8] So He knew about her faith. He also made it known that she was one *"whom Satan has bound"* and that He had loosed her. He also shared what others probably knew, that she had been trapped in this illness for eighteen years, and everyone could see that the weariness of her pain had been counteracted by the tenderness of His power. She came with her life spoiled in the grip of the Adversary, and she left renewed in the liberty of Christ. Well could she have gone home to announce, like the woman at the well, *"Come, see a Man who told me all things."*[9]

What a wonderful example she is of those whose hearts and lives are changed by the power of the gospel! Our sin unites us with her in such a definite way for the Lord *loosed her* [from *apoluō*] from her *"infirmity"* [*astheneias*], and Paul draws from both words in his letter to the Romans.

The implications of the first word are chapter 3:24, *"Being justified freely by His grace through the redemption [apolutrōsis from apoluō] that is in Christ Jesus."* This conveys the thought that believers in Christ are loosed and set free by the redemptive price of the precious blood of Christ. The second is found in chapter 5:6, *"For when we were still without strength [asthenōn and related to astheneias], in due time Christ died for the ungodly."*

The ruler of the synagogue

Had this been a company of godly people, they would have rejoiced with the woman in glorifying God for they had just witnessed the fulfilment of Matthew 8:16 — *"He cast out the spirits with a word, and healed all who were sick, that it might be fulfilled which was spoken by Isaiah the prophet, saying: 'He Himself took our infirmities and bore our sicknesses.'"* Instead, as she was released from one aspect of bondage, another revealed itself through the ruler of the synagogue who shouted out his objection without being asked. Satan had used disease in her, and now he was using his crippled mindset and of those who supported him. Typical of so many Jews, he opposed the One that is to be *"Ruler in Israel."*[10] A little bit of spiritual sensitivity would have gone a long way, but this man was shackled by his opinions. He was bound by tradition and legalism, by indifference and stubbornness, and by prejudice. By nature and nurture, he was well immersed in his bondage.

Rather than take pleasure in her healing, he showed displeasure in her being healed on the Sabbath. As is often the case with those who try to out-reason God, his reasoning turned from being rational to irrational. *"There are six days on which men ought to work."* He should have stopped there, but he tried to be too clever and stepped over the line of being reasonable by adding, *"therefore come and be healed on them, and not on the Sabbath day."* Was he really saying that any man could come and be healed on any normal working day? Was his synagogue really a place where such daily healing could take place?

Hypocrite!

This man was an unfeeling leader, unmoved and unbending, and the rigidity of his petty authority is a warning against all forms of empty formality. The Lord saw through this, and Luke records the detail of His response. Unlike many English versions, the New King James version seems to address the ruler, and then those who supported him. The Greek text reads, *"Hupokritai Hekastos humōn"* — which translates as, "Hypocrites! Each one of you." This prompted one commentary to say, "How 'the faithful and true Witness' tears off the masks which men wear!" (Jamieson, Fausset and Brown).

During the course of Luke 11 to 13, the Lord unmasked the insincerity and deception of the Pharisees' hypocrisy, but there was nothing insincere or deceitful about the woman. She takes her place among others in Luke's Gospel who glorified God —

- Shepherds - 2:20
- The man with palsy - 5:25
- The grateful leper - 17:15
- The blind man - 18:43
- The centurion - 23:47

She is a worthy addition to the list! The Lord had healed her, but He did more than that. He silenced and shamed the objectors and caused a multitude of others to rejoice in what had glorified Him. Once again, He had brought a woman to the forefront of His ministry and, by ministering so miraculously to her, God was glorified through her. She went home glorifying Him, and so did they. Her pain had turned to His praise, and now we join in the exaltation of the Saviour because of His work in her. May He do something similar through you! Annie Johnson Flint is a lovely example of a woman whose pain turned into a pleasant ministry, and we can say of her experience:

POEMS FROM PAIN

From the forge of searing heat
Ironwork is shaped and turned
Into decorative forms –
Produce of a fire that burned.
Thus the ironwork is seen
Where the burning flame had been.

From a forge of searing pain,
Gentleness as of a nurse
Turned her crippling loss to gain,
Thoughtfully expressed in verse.
Thus a ministry is seen
Where the burning fire had been.

As the iron from the heat,
So the poem from the pain;
As the ironwork was wrought,
So the verse of inward thought
Formed and shaped by unforeseen
Blessings where the fire had been.

Beneath –the hammer, blow by blow,
The anvil is unchanged below.

And be His purpose staff or sword,
His work reveals a gracious Lord.
Above – the Workman oversees
To fit whatever He may please.

Behind –the hammer, anvil too,
There burns the flame of His desire,
That He may work in me, in you,
To bring us safely through the fire,
And testify, by what is seen,
The proof of where the fire has been.[10]

Chapter 12 Questions

1. In what sort of ways has the Lord seen, called, spoken, touched and healed your life, and how do you express your spiritual profit?

2. What kind of experiences have led you to value Psalm 145:14 — *"The LORD ... raises up all who are bowed down"*?

3. How does your life reflect that God values the spiritual uprightness of His children: a) In your **prayer time** (Prov.15:8 - *"The prayer of the upright is His delight."*)? b) In your **walk**? (Ps.84:11 - *"No good thing will He withhold from those who walk uprightly."* Mic.2:7 - *"Do not my words do good to him who walks uprightly?"*)? c) In your **praise and worship** (Ps.119:7 - *"I will praise You with uprightness of heart, when I learn Your judgments."* 1 Chr.29:17 - *"I know also, my God, that You test the heart and have pleasure in uprightness. As for me, in the uprightness of my heart I have willingly offered all these things; and now with joy I have seen Your people, who are present here to offer willingly to You."*)?

Chapter 13: Phoebe

"I commend to you Phoebe our sister, who is a servant of the church in Cenchrea, that you may receive her in the Lord in a manner worthy of the saints, and assist her in whatever business she has need of you; for indeed she has been a helper of many and of myself also." (Rom.16:1,2).

I f Paul's letter to the Romans presents his appreciation of the great truths of the gospel, his closing chapter presents his great affection for those who lived by them. How fittingly it ties in with his opening greeting in chapter 1:7, where he thought of them as *"the called of Jesus Christ; to all who are in Rome, beloved of God, called to be saints"*! As sharers of the divine call, they would hear later of the glory and greatness of their calling, and, finally, receive his acknowledgement of their response to it. But his introduction also speaks of them as being *"beloved of God,"* which he would later prove in the *"us"* of His love for sinners in chapter 5:8 – *"God demonstrates His own love toward us, in that while we were still sinners, Christ died for us."* How meaningful, then, is his warm-hearted acknowledgement of those whom he describes as *"my beloved,"* as he names them in chapter 16 verses 5, 8 and 9!

I commend

In keeping with those who are called and have responded to God's call, and with those who are beloved and have responded to His love, chapter 16 begins with its own echo of what He has done. Long before its opening lines were heard for the first time, they had already heard that *"God commendeth his love toward us,"*[1] and this also was to be reciprocated by them, as Paul said, *"I commend."* Drawing from the same word, *sunistaō*, he expected the church to recognise that someone to whom God had commended His love was now being commended to them that they might be moved to show their love in return. Being *"accepted in the Beloved"*[2] should always make us accepting of each other!

Phoebe our sister

Heading up Paul's list of twenty-seven names, plus an unnamed number of fellow-saints including a mother and sister, was Phoebe from the church in Cenchrea, near Corinth. Her name means bright and shining, and was the feminine version of *Phoibos*, which was a name given to the sun god Apollo. It probably was given to her by parents who longed that she would reflect what was supposed to be the chief epithet and character of their god. Instead, she shone for the God of heaven.

These first two verses of chapter 16 are an integral part of Paul's whole letter, and they are consistent with it. There was no doubt in his mind that she shone in the brightness of one who lived up to her name, because she was among those he had already referred to as *"vessels of mercy, which He [God] had prepared beforehand for glory."*[3] Having been won to Christ from a pagan background, he valued her as *"a vessel for honour, sanctified and useful for the Master, prepared for every good work."*[4] As she absorbed this honour, she also would have been humbled by the thought, as many commentators believe, that she was not only the bearer of a letter of commendation, but of this letter to the church with his great exposition of the gospel.

On this likelihood, Donald Grey Barnhouse said, "Early tradition says that she carried the epistle to the Romans from Paul to the church in the capital. Never was there a greater burden carried by such tender hands. The theological history of the church through the centuries was in the manuscript which she brought with her. The Reformation was in that luggage. The blessing of multitudes in our day was carried in those parchments."

Leaving her home church in Cenchrea, we may wonder how long it took her to complete her journey – around seven hundred and fifty miles by sea and land – and if she had the opportunity to pore over its contents on the way. If so, she would have read Paul's commendation of her and discovered that she was bound for a church that met in various homes, as chapter 16 shows.

- The church that is in their house (v.5)
- The household of Aristobulus (v.10)
- The household of Narcissus (v.11)
- The brethren who are with them (v.14)
- All the saints who are with them (v.15)

These homes were to become her spiritual home and, although not related in the natural sense by family ties, she was about to know the spiritual bond of being a sister among them. Just as they were united locally in testimony with each other, she belonged among them as already linked with them, since her home assembly was in fellowship with *"all the churches of the Gentiles"* in verse 4. She was related to them through the call of the gospel and in every aspect of its saving truth, so this should ensure a desire to explore this great letter together. The New Testament was still in the early stages of being written, and these early Christians, in the wide range of their abilities, would learn that truths of salvation explained in chapters 1 to 11 were to become truths expressed in their lives of service.

They would grasp the practicalities of this, as chapter 12 opened up the range of spiritual gifts. Their starting point, in verse 5, was that they *"being many are one body in Christ, and individually members of one another."* This gave every brother and every sister, without exception, the assurance that unity through grace was to be shown through the diversity of their gifts. He then encouraged everyone, *"let us use them: if prophecy, let us prophecy in proportion to our faith; or ministry, let us use it in our ministering."* This is so inclusive, and well worth emphasising, that no one is excluded from enjoying what grace has given or from exercising it by faith. The secret of all their use lies in Paul's phrase, "or ministry ... in our ministering," or as the original language – *diakonian en tē diakonia* – would suggest, in a lowly deacon-like manner.

A servant of the church

Three things are mentioned about Phoebe, and the King James Version calls her a sister, a servant, and a succourer. These commend her in three distinct ways: in her relationship, in her responsibility, and in her reliability. In being commended to the church, those in Rome were being called to share in the first as fellow-saints, in the second as fellow-servants, and in the third as fellow-helpers. These go together with the fellow-workers in verses 3 and 9, the fellow-prisoners in verse 7, and with those who were fellow-labourers in verses 6 and 12. In every way, they experienced aspects of real fellowship by sharing in the corresponding realities of joy in days of prosperity and hardship in times of adversity.[5]

By referring to Phoebe as *"a servant of the church,"* Paul returns to the word *diakonos* that he has used earlier in his letter and applies it to her, but did he expect the church, or us, to understand this as a recognised office or as a commendation of her character? They had already met it in chapter 12:7 where it applies to members of the body in their gifts, and to secular officials in chapter 13:4. On this occasion they were told, *"He is God's minister"* – *Theou gar diakonos* – by which we understand from verse 1 that he belongs to authorities that *"are appointed by God"* to serve their communities. A greater example was given to them in chapter 15:8, as the Lord Jesus Christ was seen as *"a servant [diakonon] to the circumcision,"* that is to Jews. He did this, not by destroying the Law or the Prophets, but by fulfilling them,[6] and by showing Himself to be the answer to all that had been testified beforehand regarding His sufferings and subsequent glories.[7] If we confine ourselves to these three uses of the word in Romans, we can see that none of them refers to an appointed office in a church but to the character of service.

In the upper room, as the Lord showed His lowliness in the broken loaf and poured out cup before going out to Calvary, very surprisingly the disciples had *"a dispute among them, as to which of them should be considered the greatest."*[8] In response, He took the lowly place: *"I am among you as the One who serves."* What a contrast, the eternal I AM as a deacon! Other scriptures draw from the same word that it might be used of:

* Angels

At the end of forty days of temptation in the wilderness, angels were deacon-like when they *"came and ministered to Him."*[9] They had come from the ranks of heaven's innumerable host to serve Him, and angels who fulfil a lofty service Godward around the throne stooped as deacons to minister to a hungry Saviour. Even now, they fulfil a lofty service to Him above while still continuing to fulfil a lowly deacon-service toward believers on earth for are they not *"sent forth to minister for those who will inherit salvation?"*[10]

* Disciples

A disciple's journey is one of serving and following, and it's impossible to be a disciple without having the mind of a servant and a follower. The Lord links all three with His mandate: *"learn from Me"*[11] ... *serves Me* ... *follow Me,"*[12] so the journey is all about Him and the way He went. We need, therefore, to define the way He went, and have already thought of how His lowliness was expressed. Even now He reminds us that, *"The Son of Man did not come to be served* [diakonēthēnai], *but to serve* [diakonēsai], *and to give His life a ransom for many."*[13] He was the true Deacon who gave His life to serve us, and all He asks of us is that we will give our lives to serve Him.

Are we being true disciples and true followers? All we need to ask is, "Are we living as true servants?" The Lord couldn't have emphasised it more clearly than when He gave the love-hate and lose-keep option in John 12:25: *"He who loves his life will lose it, and he who hates his life in this world will keep it for eternal life."* It was then that He set out this great spiritual equation: *"If anyone serves Me, let him follow Me; and where I am, there My servant will be also. If anyone serves Me, him My*

Father will honour." Three times over, the lowliness of deaconship is shown to be the path of discipleship. John expands on this in his first letter with this pointed challenge to the claims we sometimes make: *"He who says he abides in Him ought himself also to walk just as He walked."*[14] Oh, this is more than direction, isn't it? John is stressing our need of having the same disposition. Just as disciples follow the Master, and learners follow the Teacher, so deacons should follow the Deacon. And the Father who honoured the Son will honour the servants!

> Go, labour on; spend, and be spent;
> Thy joy to do the Father's will;
> It is the way the Master went;
> Should not the servant tread it still?
> (Horatius Bonar)

In contrast to the exalted use of the word in a spiritual sense, we also find it applied secularly in the New Testament.

* Jewish workers

One example is in Matthew 22:13, in the Lord's parable of the wedding feast when a king spoke to his *"servants"* using the word *diakonois* to indicate a group of men. It was at another wedding, in connection with the first of His miracles in John 2:5, that His mother used the same word when she *"said to the servants, 'Whatever He says to you, do it.'"* On both occasions, each servant was being called to show the lowly character and willing spirit of a deacon.

* Women

One of the delightful aspects of the Lord's ministry and miracles is that women responded because they had been moved by what He said and did. On a personal level, Peter's mother-in-law was healed by His touch in Matthew 8:15, *"And she arose and served them."* In Galilee, in Luke 8:1-3, a group of women were among those who heard Jesus *"preaching and bringing the glad tidings of the kingdom of God."* Not only did He fill their hearts with hope, miraculously they were *"healed of evil spirits and infirmities,"* and with gratitude *"provided [diekonoun] for Him."* How lovely, they served Him like deacons! Having been so moved, Matthew 27:55 tells us that they followed Him to the cross – *"many women who followed Jesus from Galilee, ministering to Him, were there looking on from afar."*

They had heard His word, felt His power, and now they saw Him die. He had come to the end of His Deacon journey, and they were there – still following, and still *"ministering."* How wonderfully they were fulfilling their Saviour's words in John 12:26 for they were true disciples, true followers, and true servants! They had been united in their weaknesses, but now they were united in a different way for the word *diakonousai* means that presently, actively, plurally, a group of female deaconesses were serving Him together. And why not, since because of Him, they were united in gratitude, and in their grief, and will be in His glory!

As a servant of the church, Phoebe was a woman of their sort. From the moment of her salvation, like every born-again believer, she became a member of *"the church, which is His body"*[15] and was called to minister to others in her new deacon-like character, as we saw from Romans 12:7. Possessing this servant nature, she also became a disciple and follower of her Lord and Saviour, and, under his Lordship, showed the character of a servant in the church in Cenchrea. It was these Christlike qualities that caused Paul to commend her so positively to the church in Rome.

Other passages of Scripture help us to grasp what Paul had in mind. In Philippians 1:1 (ESV), for example, he addressed all the believers in the church and then *"the overseers and deacons."* When he wrote his first letter to Timothy, he outlined their role in chapter 3:1-13, and it is clear that he had both character and office in mind. Both of these go hand in hand in the service of a local church, since it's never the will of God that the office of either should be filled by someone who doesn't have the character. Three times in these two portions, Paul used forms of diakonos, namely *diakonois, diakonous and diakonoi*; and once the extended version as a verb, *diakoneitōsan,* which is translated as *"let them use the office of a deacon"* in the King James Version and *"let them serve as deacons"* in other versions. Either way, the previous three nouns are masculine and plural, to show that groups of men had been appointed as recognised deacons in the churches.

We noted earlier that the word *diakonousai* was used to describe the Galilean women who faithfully served the Lord, so it is interesting that there is no corresponding word used in the Acts or any of the epistles to describe the appointment of groups of deaconesses in the churches. This, in no way, takes away from women of worth having a profound effect, and the role of deacon-like women is not devalued or overlooked. On the contrary, their character is vital to the godliness and effectiveness of any gathering of the Lord's people, and this is what Paul saw in Phoebe.

That you may receive her

This was to be the warm, welcoming counterpart to Paul's commendation, and he urged the church to do it in two ways: firstly, as the Lord would; and secondly, as believers should. The strength of his appeal comes through in the word he used for *"receive"* – taking it from *prosdechomai*, which is made up of two main thoughts. The first part is *pros*, meaning toward, with the implication of facing, as in John 1:1, *"the Word was **with** God,"* indicating He was face to face with Him. The second part, from *dechomai*, means to accept. When both parts are put together, the certainty of the welcome becomes apparent for it implies, not in word only, but in genuine face-to-face acceptance of her. She was *"in Christ,"* as they were in the language of chapter 12:5, in the joy of equal security in her salvation; and she was *"in the Lord,"* in the equal opportunity and duty of her service, just as others were in chapter 16.

The church's other responsibility was to *"receive her ... in a manner worthy of the saints."* The apostle was commending her, and he expected her to be received in a commendable fashion. This is one of the God-honouring ways in which a local assembly acts in a manner that reflects its resemblance to the church, which is the body of Christ. "Saints" is a body-related relationship, along with others such as children, sheep, and members, all of which set every believer in exactly the same standing with one another.

Assist her

How appropriate it is when acceptance is confirmed by assistance! It shows that we have the same standing in Christ and that we also stand by one another in the Lord. Once again, Paul uses a word that consists of two parts – from *para*, meaning beside; and *histēmi*, which in the strong aorist and perfect tenses means to stand. The church had already heard in chapter 5:2 about their standing with each other in *"this grace in which we stand."* In this verse, he drew from the word *histēmi*, to highlight the standing we all have through the grace of God in our salvation. When both parts are put together this time, we get the added assurance that we not only share the same standing in Christ, but that the whole church would stand by Phoebe in whatever way she needed their help. Had they not been encouraged to do this in chapter 12:13? How then could they hold back from practical fellowship by *"distributing to the needs of the saints"*? By showing such love, Paul's commending and their receiving would show that she was approved, accepted, and assisted.

A helper of many

Help should always be to hand for those who need it, and it should be easiest of all to help a helper with such a reputation. She was the kind of person who saw need and made it her business to stand by those who needed help. The word used of her, *prostatis*, prominently marks her out as someone for whom others had a high regard, and this was due to the care she had for others. Many in her previous church had benefitted from her company and input to their lives and, having a real heart for people, was so sensitive and perceptive that she could see how to minister to them. This included Paul himself, and he obviously prized what she had done for him. No doubt, many women would have held back, and men too, thinking that it was beyond them to help such a distinguished person as the apostle. How well he would have known that a helpful woman is a prayerful woman, and that he would have been the subject of her prayer before he became the object of her care! And she would know that she had been moved to pray before she had been moved to help.

Down through the centuries, God has continued to move serving women, and none of them has ever been demeaned in His service. We may think of those we have never met, but have become household names in Christian circles, such as Isobel Kuhn, Gladys Aylward, Amy Carmichael and Corrie Ten Boom, and we thank God for them. But we also thank God for what we could call the unlisted legion of relatively unknown women who readily come to mind, because we can say of each one, *"She has been a helper of many and of myself also."*

Chapter 13 Questions

1. In what ways can churches make sure that sisters have ample opportunity to enjoy fulfilment in their service for the Lord?
2. All of us have the God-given opportunity to serve in deacon-like character, but how do we identify each other's gifts and get the best from one another?
3. Think of ways in which your church sets an example of fellowship by encouraging fellow-saints to be fellow servants and fellow-helpers.
4. The Lord Jesus Christ presented Himself as a deacon in His service on earth, and is now the *"Overseer of your souls"* (1 Pet.2:25) in heaven. How do you know Him as these in your life?
5. How do we develop His disposition by following Him as Master, Teacher and Deacon?

Chapter 14: Women in Church

"Greet Priscilla and Aquila, my fellow workers in Christ Jesus, who risked their own necks for my life, to whom not only I give thanks, but also all the churches of the Gentiles. Likewise, greet the church that is in their house. Greet my beloved Epaenetus, who is the firstfruits of Achaia to Christ. Greet Mary, who laboured much for us. Greet Andronicus and Junia, my countrymen and my fellow prisoners, who are of note among the apostles, who also were in Christ before me. Greet Amplias, my beloved in the Lord. Greet Urbanus, our fellow worker in Christ, and Stachys, my beloved. Greet Apelles, approved in Christ. Greet those who are of the household of Aristobulus."

"Greet Herodion, my countryman. Greet those who are of the household of Narcissus who are in the Lord. Greet Tryphena and Tryphosa, who have labored in the Lord. Greet the beloved Persis, who laboured much in the Lord. Greet Rufus, chosen in the Lord, and his mother and mine. Greet Asyncritus, Phlegon, Hermas, Patrobas, Hermes, and the brethren who are with them. Greet Philologus and Julia, Nereus and his sister, and Olympas, and all the saints who are with them. Greet one another with a holy kiss. The churches of Christ greet you" (Rom.16:3-16).

"I implore Euodia and I implore Syntyche to be of the same mind in the Lord. And I urge you also, true companion, help these women who labored with me in the gospel, with Clement also, and the rest of my fellow workers, whose names are in the Book of Life" (Phil.4:2,3).

T he first two verses of Romans 16 form Paul's commendation of Phoebe to the church in Rome, and the next fourteen read like his commendation of the church in Rome to her. As we wondered in our earlier thoughts of Phoebe, did she have opportunity to pore over the letter's contents as she travelled? If so, she must have been fascinated by this list of names, and realised that these men and women adorned what was about to become, whether for short or long, her new spiritual home. With some names embellished by Paul's varied comments, her godly mind would begin to digest the experiences through which her brothers and sisters had passed.

* Epaenetus, who is the firstfruits of Achaia

It was as if Paul gave this brother the meaning of his name by 'praising' and applauding the work of God that had been done in him. He probably was part of *"the household of Stephanas,"* since Paul referred to them in the same way – *"the firstfruits of Achaia."*[1] First converts are a memorable blessing no matter where the gospel is preached, but in these early days of the apostle's ministry among Gentiles in the southern part of Greece, Epaenetus must have been great cause for joy and thanksgiving. What an honour that the call of God through the gospel attached this special word to him!

In Leviticus 23:10, following the sacrifice of the Passover lamb, the first sheaf from the barley harvest was offered to God as *"firstfruits"* on the day after the Sabbath. It is a beautiful picture of the Saviour's death and glorious resurrection, and Paul shows it as having been fulfilled in 1 Corinthians 15:20 & 23 – *"But now Christ is risen from the dead, and has become the firstfruits of those who have fallen asleep … But each one in his own order: Christ the firstfruits, afterward those who are Christ's at His coming."* Because of His victory over sin and death, the gospel reached places such as Achaia, and Epaenetus was like an early sheaf being harvested for the Lord of the harvest. Bound in Christ, to Christ and for Christ.

* Andronicus and Junia, my countrymen and fellow prisoners

This may be a husband and wife who had suffered as Jewish believers to the extent of being imprisoned for their faith, which gave Paul a double bond with them, having been bound in the sense of Romans 9:3 as *"countrymen according to the flesh,"* and bound in prison as prisoners of the Lord.[2] They knew what it was to *"share in suffering for the gospel,"* and to *"Share in suffering as a good soldier of Christ Jesus."*[3] On these two occasions, Paul exhorted Timothy with *sungkakopatheson* from *sungkakopatheo* and implied that they shared affliction with each other for the gospel's sake. James used a related word in chapter 5:17 (RV) of his letter to say, *"Elijah was a man of like passions with us."* In his case, the word is *homoiopathēs*, which means he was a man of fellow feeling with us. Spiritually speaking, he was a true homeopath, not in the sense of the "like-treat-like" approach of alternative medicine, but in the like-with-like similarity of spiritual passion and experience.

* Amplias, my beloved in the Lord

Paul never lost the sense of endearment that belongs to being able to say, *"My little children,"*[4] and *"my true child,"*[5] and so he showed his love for *"my beloved Epaenetus."* All in the church in Rome were *"beloved of God,"* as Paul emphasised in chapter 1:7, and he expressed that love in chapter 16 to three others such as Amplias, Stachys and Persis. They had been bound in love, from God and from Paul.

This assembly was not short of love, and Phoebe was commended into its commendable church environment, knowing that Paul valued other women for their tireless service. It wouldn't go unnoticed that nine other women were mentioned, seven by name if Junia is included, so Phoebe would feel assured that she had a ministry to fulfil in Rome, as she had in Cenchrea. By speaking of them and their brethren as being *"in Christ"* and *"in the Lord,"* he also showed that Christlikeness and Lordship go together in assembly life. We have already seen from Romans 12:5 that every believer is linked *"in Christ"* as *"members of one another,"* and not as male and female as Galatians 3:28 tells us. In contrast to this, Paul told the church in 1 Corinthians 11:11, *"Nevertheless, woman is not independent of man nor man of woman, in the Lord,"* and in this God-given harmony a church fulfils its service toward God and in its community. There have been times when men have rather patronisingly said that women should know their place. It's equally true that men should know theirs, too! God's purpose is that they fulfil complementary roles to his glory.

Priscilla and Aquila

Fellowship and friendship ought to be inseparable among servants of God, though it doesn't always work out that way. Even the apostle Paul had temporary disagreements, none of which resulted in a permanent loss of fellowship. William Hendriksen makes the following observation in his commentary on Romans 16:4, "During his missionary career Paul had colleagues and fellow-workers. But he deemed it necessary to oppose Peter to his face (Gal.2:11 ff.). With Barnabas he had such a sharp disagreement that the two parted company (Acts 15:39). There was a time when Paul refused to allow Mark to remain one of his companions (Acts 15:38). He was going to reprimand Euodia and Syntyche (Phil.4:2). And Demas was going to desert him (2 Tim.4:10). But even though Prisca and Aquila in a sense stood closer to him than any others – for they were his companions both in trade and in faith – as far as the record shows, between Paul, on the one hand, and Prisca and Aquila, on the other, there was always perfect harmony" (William Hendriksen, New Testament Commentary on Romans, Banner of Truth, Reprinted 1999). For various reasons, we can see that his loving regard for them was not misplaced.

He stayed with them in Corinth, possibly for the eighteen months' duration of his visit to the church in Corinth in Acts 18:1-17. This allowed all three to form a bond of mutual closeness from which each of them benefitted. During this period, he worked with them as tentmaker, giving him a close-up view of the spiritual harmony of their lives in the home, at work, and in the church; and they of his.

He knew how fearless they were in having a church in their house, especially having returned to Rome after being deported from there by Emperor Claudius in Acts 18:2. The church in their house (see also 1 Cor.16:19) probably risked being targeted by Roman authorities, due to its inside gatherings and outside witness. One commentary says, "Aquila and Priscilla probably lived above their artisan shop. The Roman churches might especially be threatened with disunity among themselves, because Rome (unlike the cities of the East) did not allow Jews to assemble on any level larger than local synagogues, and Christians were regarded as Jews" (IVP Background Commentary: New Testament).

Such was their closeness that, in Acts 18:18, they left Corinth and sailed with him to Ephesus where they had further evidence of the reasoning and persuading that were the hallmark of his teaching in the synagogue (Acts 18:4; 19:8). Undoubtedly, their rich times of fellowship with him honed their own enjoyment of God's Word and their ability to present it. His confidence in them was shown when he continued his journey, but *"left them there"* (Acts 18:19, see also 2 Tim.4:19 for their later stay there) to continue his work with the assembly and in the synagogue.

It was in this synagogue where Paul had established a platform for the gospel that Apollos came and Aquila and Priscilla were there to vouch for his six-fold ability. He was eloquent, powerfully able in the Scriptures, instructed in the way of the Lord, spiritually on fire, his preaching and teaching were accurate, and he spoke with confidence. However, the sharp-minded couple detected a weakness, discreetly took him aside, explained the way of God more accurately to him, and through them God gave His new servant what he had been lacking. By saying, *"they took him aside and explained,"* it's clear that she was as instrumental in this as her husband. Together, they contributed to his having more to say, to being more powerfully able in the Scriptures, to being more instructed in the way of the Lord, to being more spiritually on fire, and to being more accurate in his preaching and teaching. He absorbed their exposition and went off to Achaia greatly to help believers there, knowing that eloquence, might and fervency were not enough, and well aware that increased accuracy made an essential improvement to his ministry.

The Corinthians were so impressed that they made the mistake of differentiating between each other: *"I am of Paul – I am of Apollos – I am of Cephas – I am of Christ,"*[6] He knew better, and also knew that what had been revealed to him had not come from heaven to a Damascus Road or from a Galilean beach to a fishing boat, but from a godly couple who knew how to share the Word and were ready to be used. It was after the infusion of their help that *"when he desired to cross to Achaia, the brethren wrote, exhorting the disciples to receive him; and when he arrived, he greatly helped those who had believed through grace; for he vigorously refuted the Jews publicly, showing from the Scriptures that Jesus is the Christ."*[7]

Paul also knew they had hazarded their own lives for him, putting as it were their necks on the block to prevent danger reaching him. Whether this took place in Corinth or at Ephesus is unknown, but, apart from being memorable in Paul's mind, the news became a talking point among *"all the churches of the Gentiles."*[8] In this regard, he was closing his letter in a similar manner to its opening for he had commended the whole church in chapter 1:8 by assuring them, *"I thank my God through Jesus Christ for you all, that your faith is spoken of throughout the whole world."*

Having this godly couple in a church was a real asset, and Paul was well aware that bravery and heroism flowed from their godliness and studious love for God's Word. They were true carers of God's *ekklēsia*, His community of called ones, so not only was Phoebe in good hands, his letter was too, and we can readily assume it became the focus of ardent Bible study in the church.

Tryphena and Tryphosa

Priscilla and Aquila were Paul's fellow workers or fellow labourers (*sunergous*), and the strength and reliability of their fellowship was founded upon being one in understanding of the gospel, one in the pursuit of discipleship, one in their allegiance and obedience to the faith, and one in expending energy to share what they believed. Priscilla is first in a group of sisters' names that would become fellow helpers to Phoebe, as they already had become to Paul himself. Junia, for instance, according to most English translations was a woman whom some manuscripts call Julia, and following their lead we see her as one who was treasured for being *"in Christ before* [him]." Another woman is specially marked out, not only as the mother of Rufus but as *"his mother and mine."* This isn't to suggest that he was Rufus' brother or half-brother, but to indicate the motherly care she had given him in earlier days.

John MacArthur makes a helpful comment here: "We learn from Mark's gospel, which was written after Paul wrote this letter to Rome, that Simon of Cyrene, a city on the Mediterranean coast of North Africa, who was pressed into service by the soldiers to carry Jesus' cross, was *"the father of Alexander and Rufus"* (Mk.15:21). Mark would have had no reason to include the names of Alexander and Rufus unless they were known to the church at large (through the wide distribution of Paul's letter to Rome) or at least known to the church in Rome. Scholars therefore agree that the Rufus mentioned here by Paul was one of those sons of Simon, who may have been brought to saving faith in Christ through that contact with Him on the way to Calvary. If so, he must have died before the Roman epistle was written, else he surely would have been greeted and commended by Paul.

If Simon, the man privileged to have carried Jesus' cross and to have walked beside Him to Calvary, had become a believer, he would have been among the most honored of men in the early church. It is obvious that his wife, the mother of Rufus, believed, and it seems safe to assume from this text that Alexander likewise was converted, giving reason for Mark to mention him along with his brother. Alexander either was dead or did not live in Rome at the time, else Paul would have greeted him" (MacArthur NT Commentary on Romans). Motherly, caring women will always be a blessing to God's people!

Tryphena and Tryphosa probably were younger, since Paul greets them as those *"who labour [kopiōsas] in the Lord"* (KJV) and uses the present active tense to describe their ongoing toil in service for the Lord. Their names have been translated as Dainty and Delicate, and, if this was true of them in a physical sense, they certainly overcame it in the spiritual. It's interesting to note Paul's appreciation of helpers, workers and labourers, and we may wonder if he inferred that some worked harder than others. Such a thought was probably farthest from his mind, and points more to his awareness that older ones had worked longer. This certainly is true of Persis who *"laboured much"* – *polla ekopiasen* – whose active toil was related to her past.

Robert Haldane says, "To fill any office in a church of Christ belongs only to those whom God has appointed to it; but to labour in the Gospel, either publicly or privately, is not peculiar to any office – not even to the office of an Apostle, but belongs to every Christian, according to the ability conferred on him by the Head of the Church. Christians are in general to blame for labouring so little in the Lord's service, but they can never be charged with labouring too much" (Geneva Series of

Commentaries, Romans by Robert Haldane).

As we know, Scripture has its own examples of those who failed to turn up when most needed, and they are among the things that *"were written before were written for our learning."*[9] Deborah and Barak sang, *"When leaders lead in Israel, when the people willingly offer themselves, Bless the LORD!"* They were equally aware that, although many came to the battle, others chose to stay away. This brought the justified indictment, *"Gilead stayed beyond Jordan, and why did Dan remain on ships? Asher continued at the seashore, and stayed by his inlets."*[10] Put into different words, this could be summed up as, "Gilead rested ... Dan was afraid ... Asher sat still as if married to the spot." What a difference from those of Zebulun in the next verse *"who jeopardized their lives to the point of death,* [and] *Naphtali also, on the heights of the battlefield"*! Is there not a real lesson here for us in our modern age when cruising through life and relaxing may keep us from being actively involved in the Lord's work? Yes, it's very real, and it still shows that being married to the wrong thing – hobbies, work, family, or even to our opinions – can be as damaging as being married to the wrong person.

Paul had no such fears of the church in Rome not being a welcoming and attentive spiritual home for Phoebe. Practically, they would help her in whatever reason she had come among them, and for however long. Spiritually, by means of verse 25, they were to add to her experience through their commitment *"to Him who is able to establish you according to my gospel and the preaching of Jesus Christ."* There is no doubt she would be strengthened with them as they perused what he shared in his letter of the grandeur of the gospel, and further blessed through sisters showing the value of having godly and gifted women in a church.

Euodia and Syntyche

It is very apparent that these women's relationship with each other had caused Paul's view of them to change from heart-warming to heart-breaking. He had rejoiced when, like others in Philippians 1:27, they were of *"one mind striving together for the faith of the gospel,"* but now he had to beg them *"to be of the same mind in the Lord."* With complete fairness, he addressed them individually – *"I implore Euodia and I implore Syntyche"* – so as to let each feel the weight of personal responsibility and accountability. They had been so actively involved with him in the gospel, that Paul used the word *sunēthlesan* from *sunathleō* to describe them as being like athletes together. They had been like athletic wrestlers combining their energies and complementing each other to present the way of salvation. Now they were locked in inter-personal combat competing with one another. Having been at the forefront of assembly testimony, their conduct set them at the forefront of the assembly's concern. There is nothing to suggest they had clashed over doctrinal differences, otherwise Paul would have addressed the truth of the matter. It is much more likely that something had irritated them, something that has caused them to be referred to as Odious and Soon-Touchy.

Paul had already forewarned the churches in Galatia, *"If you bite and devour one another, beware lest you be consumed one of another!"*[11] These two women were in danger of doing this to each other, but the greater danger was that, having been so prominent and respected, their divided minds would lead to others taking sides and dividing the church too. To rescue the situation, Paul's public appeal rang out: *"Help these women."* In his language, his urgency was conveyed in two words – *sullambanou autais*. The word *autais* is feminine, and he had no need to include the word 'women' as we would, since English has no way of distinguishing gender in its plural pronouns. However, where there is discord between brothers or sisters, the vital message remains, "Help them!" The mind of the Lord is that we catch them with the intention of capturing them from their animosity and cause peace and harmony to be birthed in them.

In Rome, Paul appealed for a newcomer to be received *"in the Lord"*; in Philippi, he appealed for two 'old hands' to be *"of the same mind in the Lord."* He always is the answer to His people's needs, and always the remedy for women of worth!

Chapter 14 Questions

1. When someone new becomes part of your church, how do those who are *"beloved of God"* show that they are *"beloved"* by one another?

2. While enjoying the equality that is implied by there being *"neither male nor female"* (Gal.3:28) in the church, which is the body of Christ, how do we see this in a local church where complementary roles indicate that *"neither is the woman without the man, nor the man without the woman, in the Lord"* (1 Cor.11:11 RV).

3. How can we help one another to hone the way we share the gospel in the way Paul did? In Acts 17:2-4 and 17, he *"reasoned with them from the Scriptures, explaining and demonstrating that the Christ had to suffer and rise again from the dead, and saying, "This Jesus whom I preach to you is the Christ." And some of them were persuaded"* (see Acts 18:4,19; 24:25, also regarding Apollos in Acts 18:27,28).

4. It may be straightforward to think of roles for women like Phoebe, Priscilla, Tryphena and Tryphosa, but what can be done in a church that is of a motherly nature?

5. Euodia and Syntyche's difficulty became so public that the church knew about it. What can be done to help in such a situation?

Chapter 15: Mary – the Lord's Mother

"And having come in, the angel said to her, 'Rejoice, highly favored one, the Lord is with you; blessed are you among women!' But when she saw him, she was troubled at his saying, and considered what manner of greeting this was. Then the angel said to her, 'Do not be afraid, Mary, for you have found favour with God. And behold, you will conceive in your womb and bring forth a Son, and shall call His name JESUS. He will be great, and will be called the Son of the Highest, and the LORD God will give Him the throne of His father, David. And He will reign over the house of Jacob forever, and of His kingdom there will be no end.' Then Mary said to the angel, 'How can this be, since I do not know a man?' And the angel answered and said her, 'The Holy Spirit will come upon you, and the power of the Highest will overshadow you; therefore, also, that Holy One who is to be born will be called the Son of God'" (Lk.1:28-33).

"Now there stood by the cross of Jesus His mother, and His mother's sister, Mary the wife of Clopas, and Mary Magdalene" (Jn 19:25).

"These all continued with one accord in prayer and supplication,

with the women and Mary the mother of Jesus, and with His brothers" (Acts 1:14).

J esus was the only Child who ever chose His mother. He also chose when and where He would be born, and He chose His own name. And, long before He was born, He chose when, where, how, and for whom He would die. Over seven centuries earlier, Isaiah prophesied, *"For unto us a Child is born, unto us a Son is given; and the government will be upon His shoulder. And His name will be called Wonderful [Pele'], Counselor, Mighty God, Everlasting Father, Prince of Peace."* It was a unique declaration for it captured the promise of a *"Child"* who would be *"born"* through an earthly mother, yet pre-existed as the eternal *"Son"* who would be *"given"* as co-equal with the Everlasting Father.

In former days, angels had appeared to people on earth, sometimes in person, at other times in visions, but Gabriel's visit to Nazareth was unique. No angelic message ever equalled this. The nearest, yet far from equivalent announcement, was made by the LORD when He appeared to Abraham with two angels in Genesis 18:10 and, with Sarah within earshot, promised, *"I will certainly return to you according to the time of life, and, behold, Sarah your wife shall have a son."* This certainly was divine intervention in the life of an old couple, and it was done to fulfil three aspects of divine intention: Isaac would be born, Abraham would become *"the father of all those who believe,"*[1] and that Christ would be revealed as the Seed of Abraham.[2]

Manoah and his wife in Judges 13 were another blessed couple and, this time, we are told, *"The Angel of the LORD appeared to the woman and said to her, 'Indeed now, you are barren and have borne no children, but you shall conceive and bear a son ... the child shall be a Nazirite to God from the womb; and he shall begin to deliver Israel out of the hand of the Philistines.'"*

Once again, this was divine intervention to fulfil divine intention.

Although the message came from *"the Angel of the LORD,"* many Bible students view this as a Theophany or Christophany — a pre-incarnate appearing of the Lord. Two things suggest this: in verse 18, He described His name as *"wonderful"* (*Peliy'* linked to *Pele'* for *"Wonderful"* in Isa.9:6), and *"He did a wondrous* [from the same as *Peliy'* and *Pele'*] *thing"* in verse 19. In support of this, Solomon exclaims in Psalm 72:18 *"Blessed be the LORD God, the God of Israel, who only does wondrous* [again linked to *Peliy'* and *Pele'*] *things."* The *"wondrous thing"* in Judges 13:20 was seen *"as the flame went up toward heaven from the altar—the Angel of the LORD ascended in the flame of the altar! When Manoah and his wife saw this, they fell on their faces to the ground ... And Manoah said to his wife, 'We shall surely die, because we have seen God!'"*

He and his wife watched His ascent in the flame that consumed the burnt offering, and she knew that God would not accept it and then slay them. It is such a lovely foreshadowing of the Lord Jesus ascending to heaven on the basis of His finished work of sacrifice on the cross. In due time, Samson was born to lifelong consecration as a Nazirite,[3] and, although a deliverer, He could never compare with the One of whom Mary was told, *"He shall be great,"* and confirmed to Joseph, *"He will save His people from their sins."*[4]

Blessed are you among women - Luke 1:42,43

As believers in the Lord Jesus Christ, we should enter into the meaning of this lovely commendation. Many have taken Elizabeth's words wrongly and have been led to venerate Mary as the mother of God, even to the extent of saying, "We believe that, as His mother, she can get Him to do things that His Father can't." In a reaction to this error, many others relegate her by not giving her the honour she is due, which would be overcome if we acknowledged the full extent of Elizabeth's blessing.

* In his birth

It would seem that without any mention of her coming Child, Mary's greeting caused the unborn John the Baptist to leap in Elizabeth's womb. At the same moment, she was filled by the Holy Spirit and, being led by Him, *"she exclaimed with a loud cry"* (ESV), *"Blessed are you among women, and blessed is the fruit of your womb!"* She was both empowered and enlightened by Him to recognise God's double blessing: in speaking well of Mary as the favoured vessel through whom the Saviour would be born, and that He whom she called *"my Lord"* also would be blessed in God's favour.

Mary's response is captured in her song, and we can never fail to see how it discloses her deep love for God. Her spontaneous appreciation of Him shows how richly she drew on His Word, and, while referring humbly to *"the lowly state of His maidservant,"*[5] she exalted Him as Lord and uniquely as God my Saviour before magnifying Him as mighty, holy, merciful and strong.

* In the home

If this is the place of a mother's strongest bond, it also can be the place of a family's weakest behaviour. Little is said in the four gospel accounts of homelife in Nazareth, but we know what their attitude was like as adults in John 7:3-5: *"His brothers therefore said to Him, 'Depart from here and go into Judea, that Your disciples also may see the works that You are doing. For no one does anything in secret while he himself seeks to be known openly. If You do these things, show Yourself to the world.' For even*

His brothers did not believe in Him."

This in itself may indicate that Joseph and Mary endured family conflict that may have been reflected in Joseph's situation in Genesis, *"When his brothers saw that their father loved him more than all his brothers, they hated him and could not speak peaceably to him."*[6] Jacob had years of heartache brought on by how his sons treated Joseph, and Joseph and Mary probably saw evidence of resentment toward the perfect One. From before His birth, they knew He is the *"Holy One"* incapable of sin and unworthy of blame. Can you imagine what tensions this would generate among jealous and hostile siblings?

Perhaps there's a glimpse of it in Psalm 50:20 and 21— *"You sit and speak against your brother; you slander your own mother's son. These things you have done, and I kept silent; you thought I was altogether like you."* In this regard, He may also have experienced His own words, *"a man's enemies will be those of his own household."*[7] Undoubtedly, the Lord could have said of each of His brothers, *"For as he thinks in his heart, so is he."*[8] They probably became very frustrated by the fact that He never stepped out of line and never had to be corrected. As far as Asaph, the psalmist, was concerned, the brothers he mentioned were settled in their kind of talk, as if they were married to the idea, and felt so strongly that they could slander their brother, like putting a stumbling-block in his way or pushing him over with their words. When he remained silent, they assumed he felt no need to correct them or that he condoned their language and would never hold them accountable. In truth, they were like those who said of Jeremiah, *"Come and let us attack him with the tongue."*[9]

* In His ministry

The sole purpose of the Lord's years of ministry was that, as Servant, He would glorify God and be able to say, *"I have glorified You on the earth. I have finished the work which You have given Me to do."*[10] He said this in the sure knowledge that everything had been done, and that nothing had been left undone. He also said it in anticipation of Calvary's dark hours reaching their end and being able to say, *"It is finished!"*[11] and entering *"into His glory."*[12] His three years of service had started well at the wedding in Cana of Galilee for, although changing water into wine had been a definite work by the power of God, it was His glory that was seen.[13]

The servants saw it, the master of the feast saw it, yet it was neither of them who told Him, *"They have no wine."* It was His mother, and His immediate response was, *"Woman, what does your concern have to do with Me?"*[14] She saw the need, and in the end she saw His glory, only because His whole desire was, *"I have come down from heaven, not to do My own will, but the will of Him who sent Me,"*[15] and *"I always do those things that please Him."*[16]

On a very different occasion, while replying to scribes from Jerusalem who claimed He worked by the power of Beelzebub, His mother and brothers interrupted Him. The gospel by Mark 3:31–35 sets the scene, and His reaction: *"Then His brothers and His mother came, and standing outside they sent to Him, calling Him. And a multitude was sitting around Him; and they said to Him, 'Look, Your mother and Your brothers are outside seeking You.' But He answered them, saying, 'Who is My mother, or My brothers?' And He looked around in a circle at those who sat about Him, and said, 'Here are My mother and My brothers! For whoever does the will of God is My brother and My sister and mother.'"*

Breaking off from His discourse would have meant displeasing His Father, and pleasing His mother and brothers would have meant displeasing Him by going outside the circle. So we search in vain for any occasion that allows anyone to suggest that Mary can get Him to do things that His Father can't.

* In his death

When Simeon held the Infant Jesus in his arms, he spoke personally to Mary in Luke 2:35, *"... yes, a sword will pierce through your own soul also, that the thoughts out of many hearts may be revealed."* At His final Passover time, she watched the crucifixion of her Son and this dark promise was fulfilled without Joseph at her side. The last sighting of him was in Luke 2 when he and Mary took Jesus as a twelve-year-old Boy to Jerusalem for the Passover, and left without Him. Even at that young age, when they found Him He asked, *"Why did you seek Me? Did you not know that I must be about My Father's business?"*[17]

It would seem that Joseph died prior to Jesus' death, since he was not there to care for Mary or to be involved in taking care of Jesus' body. *"Now there stood by the cross of Jesus His mother, and His mother's sister, Mary the wife of Clopas, and Mary Magdalene."* This must be one of the saddest verses in our Bibles: and so poignant, as she thought of His service beginning at a wedding and ending with His burial.

She stood at the scene, and then went home with its horror and honour forever fixed in her mind. It was over thirty-three years since she heard the shepherds acknowledge Him as *"a Saviour, who is Christ the Lord."*[18] She must often have pondered this in her heart[19] as she held the Lamb in her arms, and more so now as she saw Him as the Lamb and as the Good Shepherd on the cross.

I heard two soldiers talking
As they came down the hill —
The sombre hill of Calvary,
Bleak and black and still.
And one said, "The night is late;
These thieves take long to die."
And one said, "I am sore afraid,
And yet I know not why."
I heard two women weeping
As down the hill they came.
And one was like a broken rose,
One was like a flame.
And one said, "Now men shall rue
This deed their hands have done."
And one said only through her tears,
"My Son! My Son! My Son!"
I heard two angels singing
Ere yet the dawn was bright,
And they were clad in shining robes,
Robes and crowns of light.
And one sang, "Death is vanquished,"
And one in golden voice
Sang, "Love hath conquered, conquered all;
O Heaven and Earth, rejoice!"
(Theodosia Pickering Garrison)

* In His church

Scripture gives a detailed account in 1 Corinthians 15:5-7 of those to whom the Lord appeared after His resurrection: *"He was seen by Cephas, then by the twelve. After that He was seen by over five hundred brethren at* once ... *After that He was seen by James, then by all the apostles."* However, there is one notable silence: there is no mention that He appeared to His mother. Strangely, some have taken this silence to mean that the meeting was so private it took place before He appeared to Mary Magdalene at the tomb. This view is taken to accompany other beliefs: for instance, her bodily assumption to heaven and that she is the mother of God, views held by those who give her a place that the Word of God neither suggests nor supports. The answer may lie in her being included among the company of five hundred, since the word 'brethren' can refer to brethren and sisters together as it does later in 1 Corinthians 15:50 and 58.

What we do know is that Mary had the joy of seeing her sons' change of heart after the Lord's death and resurrection and that they were part of the gathering who responded to His command, *"tarry in the city of Jerusalem until you are endued with power from on high."*[20] Luke confirms this in Acts 1:14 — *"These all continued with one accord in prayer and supplication, with the women and Mary the mother of Jesus, and with His brothers."* We also know they married Christian women and were active in serving the Lord, for Paul asked, *"Do we have no right to take along a believing wife, as do also the other apostles, the brothers of the Lord, and Cephas?"*[21] The writings of James and Jude leave us in no doubt about their allegiance: James declaring himself to be *"a bondservant of God and of the Lord Jesus Christ,"*[22] and Jude also testifying to being *"a bondservant of Jesus Christ."*[23]

If ever men appreciated the Lord's work in reconciling them to God, these dear brothers had cause above many. They had shared their home with Him, with all those years spent out of fellowship, yet, in wondrous grace, they could look forward to Him sharing His Home with them. Mary waited long years to have the burden of her heart answered that she might witness such a change in her boys, yet, sadly, Joseph never lived to see it.

We can only speculate regarding the kind of conversations that were spawned by the interest those in the early church had about their home-life in Nazareth with Him. And well may we wonder as to what private conversations He and Mary had together during those years. John's Gospel closes with the understandable admission, *"And there are also many other things that Jesus did, which if they were written one by one, I suppose that even the world itself could not contain the books that would be written. Amen."* John probably meant this in relation to the three and a half years of His public ministry, and it would be truer still were it to include His thirty intimate years with Mary and Joseph.

The knowledge of the Holy One

John's Gospel also comes toward its end with two joint confessions. Firstly, Thomas acknowledged who Jesus is by exclaiming, *"My Lord and my God!"* in John 20:28, thus bowing to His authority and Deity. And Peter confessed His omniscience by saying, *"Lord, You know all things. You know that I love you,"* in John 21:17, meaning generally and personally.

How vital it is to know Him as God intends Him to be known. This always has been God's purpose, as encapsulated in Proverbs 9:10: *"The fear of the LORD is the beginning of wisdom, and the knowledge of the Holy One is understanding."* Earlier, in chapter 2:5, Solomon had spoken of *"the knowledge of God,"* referring to Him as *Elohim*, which is plural, meaning more than two, and consistent with His triune Person. The "Holy One" also is plural, Qᵉ*doshīm* – Holy Ones – which we understand to mean the holiness of the Father, the Son, and the Spirit. Jamieson,

Fausset and Brown's comment is, "The knowledge of the Holy is the knowledge of all that is involved in hallowing God's name; knowing experimentally all that tends to our sanctifying the Lord in our hearts and life. The parallelism to *'The fear of the LORD'* favours our taking the Hebrew Kedoshim for 'the holy God.' The same plural is used as the epithet of God in Joshua 24:19. Its plural form, like *'Elohīm* implies the Trinity in Leviticus 19:2."

Mary was never in any doubt about this. Before the beginning of His life on earth, Gabriel revealed the Triune work in her: *"The Holy Spirit will come upon you, and the power of the Highest will overshadow you; therefore, also, that Holy One who is to be born will be called the Son of God."* At the opposite end of His time on earth, with the cross behind Him, risen and ready for His ascension to heaven, Jesus urged His disciples, *"Go therefore and make disciples of all the nations, baptizing them in the name of the Father and of the Son and of the Holy Spirit."*

This has led many to speak of the Father as the first Person of the Trinity, the Son as second, and the Holy Spirit as third, and we need to ask why they draw this conclusion from Matthew 28:19 when they don't deduce from Luke 1:35 that the Holy Spirit is first, the Father second, and the Son third [see APPENDIX]. There is nothing to let us think that Mary did. She knew who He is, and who He isn't. Well might we value her willingness and submission, and be glad to be counted among those who call her blessed!

Chapter 16: Conclusion

Appending questions about home-life with the Saviour could be quite inappropriate. It's not that there is none to ask for, undoubtedly and understandably, many come to mind. There's no shortage of everyday questions —What was it like when ..? What was it like to ..? What did you do if ..? However, there would be a complete shortage of answers, since they would be based on speculation. Learning from Mary comes from following her example, not from asking questions that come like sparks from a fire fanned by curiosity. The earliest secret she applied to herself was, *"Behold the maidservant of the LORD! Let it be to me according to your word,"*[1] and her earliest secret applied to us is, *"Whatever He says to you, do it."*[2] Her mandate, *"to me ... to you,"* will guarantee a learning curve that comes from being moved by God as she was moved, according to His word. Accepting what was given to her by Gabriel as a word from God, she embraced it, being fully assured, *"The LORD is with you."*[3] It was this that strengthened her resolve to fulfil His will and deepened her understanding of Who it was that was coming into her life.

The Lord is with you

As women today who know Christ as your Lord and Saviour, God still has this to say to you — *"The Lord is with you"* — for He wants to strengthen your resolve and deepen your understanding of the One who has come into your life to stay. Mary was in no doubt: He is the *"Holy One."* As a godly Jewish girl, she knew that God Himself was the Holy One, and that the Infant to be born through her would be none other than God manifested in the flesh. As she took in the magnitude of this, scriptures that speak of the Holy One of Israel would grip her, especially since *"the knowledge of the Holy One(s) is understanding."* How her understanding would be expanded by meditating on Isaiah 54:5, and thinking of her yet unborn Child as co-equal with the One in whom Isaiah delighted! How could she not be moved?

> *"For your Maker is your husband,*
> *The LORD of hosts is His name;*
> *And your Redeemer is the Holy One of Israel;*
> *He is called the God of the whole earth."*

Perhaps you are asking the same question: "Is the same Person in me?" The answer is, "Yes, He is," so let's consider the six-fold character of the One who lives in you.

* Your Maker

Everyone who enjoys John 3:16 must do so on the basis of who John 1:1-3 says He is. The whole foundation of the gospel rests on this undeniable truth that He is God, as does His work as Creator. *"In the beginning God"* is a declaration of His eternal Being; *"In the beginning God – Elohim – created"* is a declaration that the eternal Being, as the Triune God, worked together in creation. John's Gospel opens with the revelation that nothing was made without Him, and immediately draws worship from us that this Infant is co-equal with the Maker of Isaiah 54:5. With a deep sense of added wonder we see the Son of Hebrews 1:2 given as the Child of Luke 2:17, and realise this mystery that, even then, He was *"upholding all things by the word of His power."*[4] He also is our Maker in relation to our new creation, in that only He, as God, could allow God to do a greater work —*to "make His soul an offering for sin"* (Isa.53:10) that He himself might "[make] *peace through the blood of His cross"* (Col.1:20).

> 'Twas great to speak a world from nought,
> 'Twas greater to redeem.
> (Samuel Wesley)

* Your husband

Our two previous books about 'Women God Moved' — 'Seeing the Bride in all the Scriptures' and 'Seeing the Bride in the Song of Songs' — have helped us to see the love bond in Israel's bridal relationship with God. In a similar way, we have been able to see the love bond that we enjoy in the bridal relationship between the Lord Jesus Christ and His church. God's purpose in the Passover that led to Israel's bridal bond being formed through the Law and through the lamb, were a lovely foreshadowing of bringing a bride as the wife of the Lamb[5] in His purpose and grace through the cross.

* The LORD of Hosts

Fleeing to Egypt in the care of Joseph and Mary in Matthew 2:13-15 hardly gives the impression that the Child, as co-equal Creator and Upholder, had equality with God as *Yahweh Ts^{e}ba'ōt*, LORD of Hosts.

Nevertheless, Matthew is quick to point out that God was more intent with fulfilling His word through Hosea 11:1, *"Out of Egypt I called My Son."* Formerly understood as applying to His people's release from Egypt's bondage, Matthew disclosed its real fulfilment was in God's own Son being brought out. At the end of His days on earth, when Peter drew his sword to defend the Lord in Gethsemane, he was asked, *"Do you think that I cannot now pray to My Father, and He will provide Me with more than twelve legions of angels?"*[6] It was a clear way of demonstrating that His equality as LORD of Hosts didn't depend on marshalling them, but in having access to them. Once again, He didn't, and for exactly the same reason: *"How then could the Scriptures be fulfilled, that it must happen thus?"* Fulfilling His purpose was more important than enforcing His power.

* Your Redeemer

It was for this reason He had come, that His power as Redeemer would be made known only through His submission to death, and not by any other means of protection. By divine permission, angels were allowed to attend His incarnation,[7] His temptation,[8] and before and after His crucifixion,[9] but a greater power than their combined forces must redeem – the power of His own redeeming blood.

> Would you be free from your burden of sin?
> There's power in the blood, power in the blood;
> Would you o'er evil a victory win?
> There's wonderful power in the blood.
> (Lewis E. Jones)

* The Holy One

When a newly redeemed host sang with Moses their mediator, they rejoiced in God who had *"triumphed gloriously"* and is *"glorious in holiness."*[10] We catch the enthralment of their praise in these words, *"He has triumphed gloriously"* — *gā'oh gā'āh.* Adam Clarke helps us with the meaning of this by adding, "He is exceedingly exalted" ... "He is gloriously glorified"; and surely this was one of the most signal displays of the glorious majesty of God ever exhibited since the creation of the world. And when it is considered that the whole of this transaction foreshadowed the redemption of the human race from the bondage and power of sin and iniquity by the Lord Jesus ... we may also join in the song, and celebrate Him who triumphed so gloriously."

After healing the lame man at the gate of the temple, Peter reasoned with the people in Acts 3:12-16:

> *"So when Peter saw it, he responded to the people: 'Men of Israel, why do you marvel at this? Or why look so intently at us, as though by our own power or godliness we had made this man walk? The God of Abraham, Isaac, and Jacob, the God of our fathers, glorified His Servant Jesus, whom you delivered up and denied in the presence of Pilate, when he was determined to let Him go. But you denied the Holy One and the Just, and asked for a murderer to be granted to you, and killed the Prince of life, whom God raised from the dead, of which we are witnesses. And His name, through faith in His name, has made this man strong, whom you see and know. Yes, the faith which comes through Him has given him this perfect soundness in the presence of you all.'"*

The force of his message was that by rejecting Jesus, the unwanted Man, they had rejected the unwanted God whose names Jesus shared. He also is the Holy One and, through the work of His cross, He had gloriously glorified Him.

* The God of the whole earth

Maker, Husband, LORD of Hosts, Redeemer, Holy One: our Lord and Saviour Jesus Christ is all of these, the reason being He also is God of the whole earth. Under the Old Covenant, the ark in the tabernacle's Most Holy Place was a unique symbol of the Holy One glorified in the presence of His God and Father. It had been formed under the supreme skill of Bezalel[11] whose name means 'in the shadow of God,' but when it became time for the Holy One to be born, who is God manifest in the flesh, this took the Divine genius of the power of the Most High through a woman. God's command regarding the ark was, *"When you see the ark of the covenant of the LORD your God ... then you shall set out from your place and go after it."*[12] He has different names, as we have thought, so also did the ark that His people might relate to its sevenfold message.

1. The ark of God - **DEITY**
2. The ark of the God of Israel - **IDENTITY**
3. The ark of the covenant of the LORD - **AUTHORITY**
4. The ark of the covenant of the LORD of all the earth - **SECURITY**
5. The ark of Your strength - **ABILITY**
6. The ark of the testimony - **VERACITY**
7. The holy ark - **PURITY**

Had you been there, would these have been enough to make you *"go after it"*? God gave each person among His people a wonderful reason to *"set out from your place,"* yet He has given us one that is better. The Lord

Jesus Christ has called us to follow Him and, no matter what may have held you back until now, He is asking if you are ready to *"set out from your place."* Just as He leads men of God, so He also leads women of God. He is worthy of your best, and, is calling you to rise and *"go after* [Him]*."* All the women we have thought about had a God-given opportunity to respond, and you do, too, that you might have the honour of being included among the 'Women God Moved.'

I heard Him call —
"Come, follow," that was all.
My gold grew dim
My soul went after Him
I rose and followed, that was all.
Who would not follow
If they heard Him call?
(Henry Wadsworth Longfellow)

Appendix

Over the centuries, different churches have held three different views of God. The Unitarian view is that God consists of one Person; the Binitarian view is that He consists of two Persons – the Father and the Son; and the Trinitarian belief is of a triune Person – the Father, the Son, and the Holy Spirit. Sometimes, within the Trinitarian view, the Holy Spirit is referred to as the third Person of the Trinity, and the Lord Jesus Christ is said to be the second Person of the Trinity. We do not suggest that they intentionally question Their mutual Deity, equality or sovereignty, but, unintentionally, they may infer there is inequality or inferiority among Them. For this reason, we apply briefly to Scripture for clarification regarding whether any particular order is intended.

As we have already said, Matthew 28:19 speaks of the Father, the Son, and the Holy Spirit, which may lead some to regard the Father as first, the Son second, and the Holy Spirit third. We could, however, take Romans 8:11, which says, *"But if the Spirit of Him who raised Jesus from the dead dwells in you,"* we will see that the Spirit is first, the Father is second, and the Son is third. If we turn to 2 Corinthians 13:14, we will read, *"The grace of the Lord Jesus Christ, and the love of God, and the communion of the Holy Spirit be with you all. Amen."* Now the Son is first, the Father second, and the Spirit third. Another change can be found in Hebrews 9:14, which speaks of, "the blood of Christ, who through the eternal Spirit offered Himself to God," and we note that the Son is first, the Spirit is second, and the Father is third. Jude 20 and 21 urges us, *"praying in the Holy Spirit, keep yourselves in the love of God, looking for the mercy of our Lord Jesus Christ."* Like Romans 8:11, the Holy Spirit is first, the Father is second, and the Son is third. If we take all these verses together, they help us to see Their equality in Deity rather than any suggestion that the variation in textual order ever implies any superiority or inferiority within the Trinity.

Scripture also helps us to see They are One in —

Holiness

- Holy God (Father) – Lev.11:44,45; 1 Pet.1:15,16
- Holy One (Son) – Mk.1:24; Acts 2:27; 3:14
- Holy Spirit – Jn 14:26; Matt.3:16; Phil. 1:19

Glory

- God of glory (Father) – Acts 7:2
- Lord of glory (Son) – 1 Cor 2:8
- Spirit of glory – 1 Pet.4:14

Name

- Father, Son and Holy Spirit – Matt 28:19 ('the Name' is singular, combining all Three)

It also helps us to see that They work as One in:

- Creation (Gen.1:1; Gen.1:2; Jn 1:3; Col.1:16)
- Incarnation (Lk.1:35)
- Baptism (Matt.3:16,17)
- Crucifixion (Heb.9:14)
- Salvation (1 Jn 4:14; Gal.2:20; 2 Thess.2:13)
- Benediction (2 Cor.13:14)

Acknowledged by Deity, Disciples and Demons

As to the Lord Jesus Christ Himself, His Father attested His deity on His return to heaven: *"Your throne, O God, is forever and ever; a scepter of righteousness is the scepter of Your kingdom. You have loved righteousness and hated lawlessness; therefore God, Your God, has anointed You with the oil of gladness more than Your companions."*[1] In absolute equality, the Father addressed the Son as God, and also refers to Himself as God, so they mutually adore each other as God.

When the Lord asked His disciples regarding His true identity, Peter's satisfactory answer was, *"You are the Christ, the Son of the living God."*[2] The Lord's reply was that Peter had learned this by revelation from *"My Father who is in heaven."* He could have said, "Your God who is in heaven," but He emphasised that the Father-Son relationship was Theirs as God, just as They mutually reveal each other in Matthew 11:25-27. With Calvary over and appearing to His disciples for the second time, Thomas addressed Him as *"My Lord and my God!"*[3] Later Paul wrote to Titus about *"our great God and Saviour Jesus Christ,"*[4] so His Deity was fully accepted among His disciples.

In Mark 1:24 and 25, demons cried out in chorus from a demon-possessed man, *"What have we to do with You, Jesus of Nazareth? Did You come here to destroy us? I know who You are— the Holy One of God!"* How did demons know that "Jesus of Nazareth" was the earthly name of this heavenly Person who is "of God"? Unlike Peter, it was because he and his fellow-demons had come from heaven where they had seen Him before they were cast out. Unknown to those in the synagogue, this is what lay behind their questioning surprise: *"What is this? What new doctrine is this? For with authority He commands even the unclean spirits, and they obey him."* As the Holy One of God, He had cast them out of heaven; and now, as possessor of that Name, He had power as Jesus of Nazareth to cast them out of a man on earth!

Who Jesus is, and who He isn't

Among the lovely presentations of the Lord Jesus Christ in His Word are names and titles that have a numerical association. He is *"the First"* or *"the Alpha"* in Revelation 1:11; He is *"the second Man"* in 1 Corinthians 15:47; He is one of *"three men"* who appeared to Abraham in Genesis 18:1, 2; He is the *"fourth"* man in Daniel 3:25; and He is *"The last Adam"* in 1 Corinthians 15:45 and *"the Last"* of Revelation 1:11. These all speak of who Jesus is, though someone may unintentionally misquote *"The last Adam"* and call Him the second Adam. Important as this is, since there will never be a third, it is easily resolved. What is more difficult to resolve is the intentional reference to the Lord as the second Person or to the Holy Spirit as the third Person of the Trinity for it is not always intended to imply that They are not co-equal as God with God. The Scriptures do not show that They eternally pre-existed as second and third Persons, and there is no indication that They ever became so. There is perfect order in the Trinity, but nothing to indicate an order. They are Three-in-one and One-in-Three, yet nowhere are they presented as first, second, and third. God has graciously called us *"to know [Him] the only true God, and Jesus Christ whom [He has] sent,"*[5] so we want to know who He is, and who He isn't.

What think you of Christ?

What think you of Christ? is the test
To try both your state and your scheme;
You cannot be right in the rest,
Unless you think rightly of Him.

As Jesus appears in your view,
As He is beloved or not;
So God is disposed to you,
And mercy or wrath are your lot.

Some take Him a creature to be,
A man, or an angel at most;
Sure these have not feelings like me,
Nor know themselves wretched and lost:

So guilty, so helpless, am I,
I durst not confide in His blood,
Nor on His protection rely,
Unless I were sure He is God.

(John Newton)

REFERENCES

Chapter 2: Sarah

(1) Gen.3:15 (2) Gal.3:16 (3) Rom.1:3 (4) Isa.51:2 (5) Heb.11:17-19 (6) Eph.3:16,17 (7) Jas.1:21 (8) Col.3:16 (9) Gen.20:12 (10) Gen.21:6,7 (11) Jas.5:11 (12) Job 2:9 (13) Isa.41:8; Jas.2:23 (14) Gen.18:17 (15) See Chapter 5 of 'Men God Moved – The Apostle Jude's Tripod' published by Hayes Press, 2019 – ISBN 9781789101935 (16) Gen.12:1; Acts 7:2,3 NASB (17) 2 Pet.1:4 (18) Rom.6:14 (19) Phil.2:12 (20) Heb.12:14 (21) 1 Pet.1:16 (22) Ex.3:14 (23) Rom.2:4 (24) 2 Cor.7:8-12 (25) Gal.3:29 (26) Tit.2:10

Chapter 3: Overlooked Women – Part 1

(1) Adam Clarke's Commentary (2) Matthew by J. Heading – What the Bible Teaches (3) 1 Pet.3:7 (4) Rom.5:6 ESV (5) Prov.21:1 (6) Prov.19:21 RV (7) Ps.76:10 (8) Ex.2:9 (9) Jas.3:15,17 (10) Job 26:13 (11) Ps.8:3 (12) Ps.33:9 (13) Rom.3:10-12 (14) Matt.11:29 RV (15) 2 Cor.7:1 (16) Col.3:23-24 ESV (17) Deut.12:25 (18) Gen.4:7 (19) Heb.11:6

Chapter 4: Overlooked Women – Part 2

(1) Matt.6:6 (2) 2 Chron.7:14 (3) Prov.16:3 (4) Prov.4:26 RVM (5) Prov.16:2 (6) Prov.21:2 (7) 1 Sam.2:3 (8) Ezra 9:12 (9) Obad.17 (10) 2 Chron.20:11 (11) Ps.83:12 (12) Rev.15:3 ESV (13) Rom.2:4 (14) Rom.9:23

(15) Eph.1:7 (16) Heb.9:15 (17) Rom.6:23 (18) Eph.3:11 (19) Isa.14:24 (20) Jn 19:30 (21) Eph.1:11,14 (22) Rom.10:17 (23) Ps.40:2,3 (24) Rom.8:13 (25) Gal.5:16 (26) 1 Thess.4:1 (27) Rom.5:2

Chapter 5: Deborah

(1) Judg.2:17,18 (2) Judg.3:11,12,30;4:1,2; 10:1-6 (3) Judg.3:8,12:4:2 (4) Judg.4:6-8 (5) 1 Kin.22:7 NIV (6) Judg.7:10 (7) Isa.12:2 (8) Job 29:7 (9) Judg.5:7 ESV (10) 1 Cor.4:15 (11) 1 Kin.2:2 (12) Judg.4:6 (13) Josh.20:7; Gen.30:8 (14) Judg.5:20 (15) Jer.17:12 ESV (16) 1 Cor.14:20 KJV (17) Rom.8:3 (18) Rom.8:7 (19) Gen.3:15 (20) Matt.12:18 (21) Jn 1:1 (22) 1 Cor.1:18 ESV (23) Ps.62:11 (24) Ps.89:12,13 (25) Ps.104:3 (26) Isa.46:11 (27) Lam.2:17 (28) Isa.29:14; 1 Cor.1:19,20 (29) 1 Pet.3:7 (30) 1 Cor.1:27

Chapter 6: Abigail

(1) Prov.19:14 (2) Rom.9:6 (3) Num.14:24 (4) Gen.39:6 KJV (5) 1 Sam.17:11 (6) Gen.32:20 (7) Matt.12:34 (8) Ruth 1:20 (9) 1 Sam.25:24-27, 28-31

Chapter 7: A Certain Woman

(1) 2 Chron.20:15 (2) 2 Chron.20:17 (3) 2 Kin.3:20 ESV (4) Ex.29:38-40 (5) Lev.25:11,40 (6) Ps.55:18 (7) Ps.86:11 (8) Matt.15:32; Mk.6:36 (9) Lk.5:5; Jn 21:3 (10) 2 Cor.6:10 (11) Rev.2:9 (12) 2 Cor.8:2 (13) Ps.146:9 (14) Acts 10:13,14 (15) Jer.49:11 (16) Ps.68:5 (17) Tit.3:5,6

Chapter 8: A Notable Woman

(1) 1 Pet.5:5 (2) Eph.4:12 ESV (3) Eph.3:6 RV (4) 1 Tim.6:6 (5) Phil.2:8 RSV (6) 2 Kin.17:13 (7) Gal.3:5 (8) Jn 4:16 (9) Eccl.4:8,9,12 (10) Lk.7:15 NASB

Chapter 9: Choice Women

(1) Prov.15:3 (2) 2 Cor.5:10 (3) Rom.14:12 ESV (4) Josh.6:25 RV (5) Prov.25:19 (6) Ps.119:63 (7) Ex.26:9,12 (8) Jn 10:10 (9) 2 Cor.8:7 (10) 1 Thess.4:1 (11) Lk.2:25 (12) Lk.2:38 (13) 2 Cor.8:5 (14) 1 Cor.15:58 (15) 1 Cor.11:11

Chapter 10: Building Women

(1) Eccl.3:3 (2) Ezra 1:1 (3) Isa.44:28 (4) Prov.21:1 (5) Neh.2:10 (6) Neh.4:2 (=3:34, Heb.) (7) Neh.4:10 (=4:4, Heb.) (8) Neh.4:9 (=4:3, Heb.) (9) Neh.4:15 (=4:9, Heb.) (10) Neh.3:5,27 (11) Neh.4:23 (= 4:17, Heb.) (12) Neh.6:15 (13) Heb.10:25 (14) Rom.10:9 ESV (15) 2 Pet.3:18 (16) 2 Pet.1:10,11 (17) Ruth 2:12 (18) Lk.22:32 (19) Acts 15:32 (20) Rev.3:2 (21) 1 Pet.5:10 NIV (22) Neh.8:3 (23) Neh.8:9 (24) Acts 20:31 (25) 2 Tim.1:3,4 (26) Lk.7:44

Chapter 11: The Woman at the Well

(1) Acts 3:15 ESV (2) Isa.9:6 (3) Acts 3:13 (4) Jn 8:58 (5) Isa.1:19 (6) Matt.11:27 (7) Deut.18:18 (8) Acts 3:26 (9) Jer.17:10 (10) Matt.11:28 (11) Acts 26:18 (12) Acts 3:19-20 ESV (13) Col.1:13 (14) Rom.2:4 (15) 1 Jn 3:9 (16) Jn 6:37,44 (17) Eph.2:11-14 (18) Jn 8:24

Chapter 12: An Infirm Woman

(1) Zech.12:10 (2) Isa.35:6 (3) Isa.50:4 (4) Psa.113:5-7 (5) Job 31:4 (6) Jn 6:6 (7) Gen.1:16 (8) Lk.19:9 (9) Jn 4:29 (10) Mic.5:2 (10) Written by AMcI for the Preface of her republished poems by Hayden Press, 2019.

Chapter 13: Phoebe

(1) Rom.5:8 KJV (2) Eph.1:6 (3) Rom.9:23 (4) 2 Tim.2:21 (5) Eccl.7:14
(6) Matt.5:17 (7) 1 Pet.1:11 (8) Lk.22:24 (9) Matt.4:11 (10) Heb.1:14 (11)
Matt.11:29 (12) Jn 12:26 (13) Matt.20:28 (14) 1 Jn 2:6 (15) Eph.1:22,23

Chapter 14: Women in Church

(1) 1 Cor.16:15 (2) Eph.4:1 (3) 2 Tim.1:8; 2:3 ESV (4) Gal.4:19 (5) 1 Tim.1:2;
Tit.1:4 RV (6) 1 Cor.1:12 (7) Acts 18:27,28 (8) Rom.16:4 (9) Rom.15:4 (10)
Judg.5:17 (11) Gal.5:15

Chapter 15: Mary – the Lord's Mother

(1) Rom.4:17 (2) Gal.3:16 (3) Num.6 (4) Matt.1:21, Lk.1:15 5. Lk.1:48 (6)
Gen.37:4 (7) Matt.10:36 (8) Prov.23:7 (9) Jer.18:18 (10) Jn 17:4 (11) Jn
19:30 (12) Lk.24:26 (13) Jn 2:11 (14) Jn 2:3,4 (15) Jn 6:38 (16) Jn 8:29 (17)
Lk.2:49 (18) Lk.2:11 (19) Lk.2:19 (20) Lk.24:49 (21) 1 Cor.9:5 (22) Jas.1:1
(23) Jude 1

Chapter 16: Conclusion

(1) Lk.1:38 (2) Jn 2:5 (3) Lk.1:28 (4) Heb.1:3 (5) Rev.19:7 (6) Matt.26:53
(7) Lk.2:10-14 (8) Matt.4:11 (9) Lk.22:43; Jn 20:12 (10) Ex.15:1,11 (11)
Ex.37:1-9 (12) Jos.3:3

Appendix

(1) Heb.1:8,9 (2) Matt.16:16 (3) Jn 20:28 (4) Tit.2:13 (5) Jn 17:3

ABOUT THE AUTHOR

Andy was born in Glasgow, Scotland, He came to know the Lord in 1954, and was baptized in 1958. He is married to Anna, and he lives in Kilmacolm, Scotland. They have two daughters and one son. He entered into full-time service in 1976 with the churches of God (www.churchesofgod.info). He has engaged in an itinerant ministry in western countries and has been privileged to serve the Lord in India and Myanmar (formerly Burma).

MORE BOOKS FROM THE AUTHOR

Grace in First Peter - The Many-Splendoured Grace Shown to an Ungracious Man (Men God Moved - Book One)

As Andy says, "Tracing the grace of God in Peter's first letter is like seeing the glory of God in Romans and the greatness of God in Hebrews." In this deeply practical book, Andy takes us through each of Peter the rough fisherman's 5 chapters, and introduces us to the manifold grace of God expressed in at least 11 different aspects:

1. GRACE REQUIRED IN AN UNGRACIOUS MAN
2. GRACE RESTORED IN OUR MISTAKES
3. GRACE RECEIVED IN THE GOSPEL
4. GRACE REGARDED IN WORSHIP AND WITNESS
5. GRACE REINFORCED IN TRIALS
6. GRACE RECIPROCATED IN MARRIAGE
7. GRACE RECOGNISED IN HOLINESS
8. GRACE REVEALED IN SPIRITUAL GIFTS
9. GRACE REFLECTED IN LEADERSHIP
10. GRACE REGAINED IN BIBLICAL TRUTH
11. GRACE RE-EMPHASISED IN PAUL'S LETTERS

The Apostle Jude's Tripod - The Man, Method and Message of the New Testament's Forgotten Book (Men God Moved - Book Two)

The apostle Jude's little letter can easily be read within five minutes, yet it spans eternity past and future, history and prophecy, blessing and judgment, past revelation and fresh revelation, things known and not known, heaven's glory and hell's grief. And, like all Scripture, it has a God-given relevance for us in the present day:

* for reproof – showing when we are off track
* for correction – helping us to get back on track
* for instruction – enabling us to keep on track.

As Jude wrote his little book, it's as if he did so with the mindset of a surveyor, scanning the worrying spiritual landscape in front of him - 19 times in his short letter, Jude moves his surveyor's 'tripod' of threes to drive his point home. In addition to exploring each of these, Bible teacher Andy McIlree unpacks each verse across seven key themes of Salutation, Salvation, Contention, Condemnation, Revelation, Benediction and Doxology.

This is a very enlightening and practical study of a little understood, under-appreciated and often forgotten part of our New Testament.

Boaz - Ruth's Redeemer, Bridegroom and Lord of the Harvest (Men God Moved - Book Three)

The events of the book of Ruth are like a jewelled cameo woven into the fabric of Israel's chequered background. The account of Ruth's arrival on the pages of God's Word is an interweaving of His grace, His call – so typical of His reaching out to Abraham, Rahab, and to Gentiles – and His purpose. So, during Israel's dull days, she is like a colourful butterfly emerging from a very drab chrysalis.

There is no shallow end to the story of Ruth, as depths of despair at the beginning lead on to deepening delight, which causes us to exclaim, "Oh, the depth of the riches both of the wisdom and knowledge of God! How unsearchable are His judgments and His ways past finding out!"

Join Bible teacher Andy McIlree in this heart-warming study as, chapter by chapter, he explores the depths of this wonderful Old Testament book, and in particular how Boaz is a picture of the Lord Jesus as our kinsman-redeemer, bridegroom and the Lord of the harvest.

Seeing the Bride in All the Scriptures (Women God Moved - Book One)

After looking at Peter, Jude and Boaz as 'Men God Moved' who were stirred and carried along by the Holy Spirit to fulfil God's purpose, Andy turns to look at 'Women God Moved' to see how He also used them: some, by their godly example; others, because of the imagery conveyed by the place they occupy in His Word.

Along with everything God wants us to gain from this study, Christian women should be assured that He never devalues them. To prove this,

He has used a series of Bible brides to occupy very special places in His purpose, and emphasise that He elevates them to the highest possible level by using them as examples of what He calls "the bride, the Lamb's wife." Andy begins in Genesis and continue in the Books of the Law, before flowing on through the Psalms and the Prophets - and looks at Eve, Rebekah, Israel, the Shulamite, Ruth and more.

At the outset, Andy acknowledges that we have the right to explore the Word, but clear pictures will not emerge unless we give the Lord the right to explain. When He does, the effect on us ought to mirror how the two from Emmaus felt when they asked, "Did not our heart burn within us while He talked with us on the road, and while He opened the Scriptures to us?" May ours be the same!

Seeing the Bride in the Song of Songs (Women God Moved - Book Two)

In this second book of the series, Andy explores the often neglected Song of Songs. Some question whether it should be in the Bible at all, while many have struggled to understand the purpose of its poetic imagery. But there's no need to be afraid of this very human and very devotional book, that has been described by one Jewish rabbi as the holiest of all of Israel's scriptures.

It's a sequence of love letters between a young couple, expressed in words and behaviour that would have been so meaningful to them, although they may at first seem peculiar to us today. Andy invites us to allow its language to first of all lift our thoughts to see God being exalted in His relationship with His people, Israel; these eight chapters is displayed the supremacy of God, clothed in His fervency and intimacy

– and even under Law, His working with His people had much grace blended with it. Then, on another level, His Spirit can exalt His Son as we draw lessons that relate to our walk with Him. God has included this Song in His Word for our good, so that He may share with us something from "the exceeding riches of His grace in his kindness toward us in Christ." May we allow the Holy Spirit to interpret and apply the beauties of this allegory richly to our Christian lives, until truths become evident that will shape the course of our spiritual will and our discipleship walk.

The Five Solas of the Reformation

Five centuries after Luther nailed his Ninety-five Theses to the door of a Catholic church, is there still a need for reformation? Yes, the Reformers' 'Five Solas' - Scripture Alone, Christ Alone, Grace Alone, Faith Alone, the Glory of God Alone - should be engraved on all our hearts, and the need could hardly be greater for them to be nailed to the doors of today's shallow churches today that are in danger of "being destroyed for lack of knowledge" (Hosea 4:6).

Garments for Glory

This book is an indispensable in-depth study of the types and shadows (pictures) of Christ in Israel's High Priest under the Levitical Order of the Old Testament Tabernacle and Temple, and specifically how his work, person and clothing speak of Jesus as our Great High Priest on the throne of God. But this is far from a dry, scholarly endeavour; its meditations will make your heart soar in fresh appreciation of what God has so expertly revealed in His Word about His Son; and its challenges will help you consider afresh "how should we now live" in view of what God has revealed to us about His Son.

ABOUT THE PUBLISHER

Hayes Press (www.hayespress.org) is a registered charity in the United Kingdom, whose primary mission is to disseminate the Word of God, mainly through literature. It is one of the largest distributors of gospel tracts and leaflets in the United Kingdom, with over 100 titles and many thousands dispatched annually. In addition to paperbacks and eBooks, Hayes Press also publishes Plus Eagles' Wings, a fun and educational Bible magazine for children, and Golden Bells, a popular daily Bible reading calendar in wall or desk formats.

If you would like to contact Hayes Press, there are a number of ways you can do so:

By mail: c/o The Barn, Flaxlands, Royal Wootton Bassett, Wiltshire, UK SN4 8DY

By phone: 01793 850598

By eMail: info@hayespress.org

via Facebook: www.facebook.com/hayespress.org